D. Caroline Coile, Ph.D.

Miniature Pinschers

Everything About Purchase, Care, Nutrition, Behavior, and Training

Filled with Full-color Photographs
Illustrations by Michele Earle-Bridges

BARRON'S

CONTENTS

THE INIMITABLE MIN PIN

The Miniature Pinscher is one of a kind. Rambunctious, impetuous, and oh so very busy, the Miniature Pinscher (more affectionately known as the Min Pin) is the dog world's answer to the perpetual motion machine.

The Min Pin's Past

The Miniature Pinscher is not a miniature version of the Doberman Pinscher. In fact, the Miniature Pinscher is the older of the two breeds. Although the two breeds resemble each other superficially, that resemblance probably stems in part from their common relation to the German Pinscher, an older yet now comparatively rare breed intermediate in size between the two.

The Miniature Pinscher is both an ancient and a modern breed—ancient because it descends from terrier-type dogs indigenous to Germany for many centuries, but modern because its present form is derived from the purposeful interbreeding of several breeds in the early nineteenth century.

The Miniature Pinscher is a product of early nineteenth-century Germany.

The ancient terriers came in both medium and small sizes, and in both smooth and wire (and sometimes long) coats. These feisty dogs were adept at dispatching vermin, and even today, their descendants are apt and fearless hunters. Because of the emphasis upon function, the sizes and coat types were commonly interbred as late as the eighteenth century. However, as interest in specialized pure breeds grew, the types eventually were separated and became the foundation for many of the modern-day breeds, including the Miniature Pinscher.

Clues about the Miniature Pinscher's development are scarce, but it is noteworthy that as early as 1640 a small cat-sized red dog, fine boned and with prick ears, is depicted in a painting of a peasant family. It is likely that this represents one of the small short-haired terriers rather than a distinct breed, however. Later paintings from the 1800s include dogs of distinctly Miniature Pinscher type.

Crossbreeding: Although it cannot be documented, it is believed that the Miniature Pinscher resulted from the crossing of the small short-haired terrier with the Dachshund and the Italian Greyhound. Many of the traits of these original breeds can be seen in today's Miniature Pinschers: the feistiness, strong body structure, and black and tan coloration of the German Pinscher; the fearlessness and clear red coloration of the Dachshund; and the playfulness, elegance, and lithe movement of the Italian Greyhound. But there is no accounting for the sheer energy level and inquisitive nature of today's Miniature Pinschers!

These little German spitfires were developed into a distinct breed, the "Reh Pinscher," in the early 1800s. The reh is a small red German deer (or roe deer), which the little dog was thought to resemble, and Pinscher simply means terrier, which is an accurate reflection of its feisty ancestry.

German breeds: German breeds of dog have earned the reputation of being some of the most finely bred dogs in the world. Their standards of perfection are exacting, and their criteria for breeding are stringent. The reh Pinscher was no exception. The early (late 1800s) emphasis upon breeding the tiniest Miniature Pinscher, with no regard for grace or soundness of movement or body, threatened to result in a race of diminutive cripples with bulging eyes. Luckily, this trend was reversed, so that by the time the breed was awarded official breed recognition in 1895, the foundation for the elegant, agile, strong-bodied Miniature Pinschers as they are known today was clearly discernible.

Pre-World War I: This modern-type Miniature Pinscher quickly became one of the most popular and well-developed show dogs in pre-World War I Germany, but following the war there the German Min Pin experienced a plunge in both numbers and quality. Fortunately, the breed had been exported and was gaining fans abroad, including in America, where it received American Kennel Club (AKC) recognition in 1929 as a member of the toy group.

Today: Since that time, the Miniature Pinscher has slowly accumulated an almost fanatically loyal following. With careful breeding, the breed has become more elegant, refined, and graceful, without sacrificing its strength and vitality. Today's Min Pin is lively, animated, feisty, and independent. Its sleek lines, lithe and supple body, and high-stepping hackney prance make it an eye-catcher in any crowd. One look at a Min Pin surveying its domain and there is

Despite appearances, the Miniature Pinscher is not a bred-down Doberman Pinscher.

no question why it has been dubbed the "king of toys."

Miniature Pinschers have long been a favorite of dog show exhibitors. With their natural "look-at-me" attitude, they are show dogs par excellence. But more recently, they have attracted the attention of families interested only in having an elegant showstopper in their own home. Pet owners have discovered that the Miniature Pinscher can be an alert watchdog, a lively companion, and an untiring clown.

But as the Min Pin grows in popularity, many people are drawn to the breed without fully understanding the minuses as well as the pluses of having a whirling dervish in their homes.

Is the Min Pin for You?

Temperament

Most people are initially attracted to a breed because of its looks, and the dapper little Min Pin is undeniably stunning. No breed of dog—absolutely no breed—can compete with the Min Pin when it comes to strutting, prancing, and standing at attention. But have you ever seen a Min Pin at rest? (Yes, they do sleep, but most Min Pins have to fit sleep into a very busy calendar.) Many people find this constant activity to be one of the most enchanting and entertaining attributes of the breed; others find it unnerving or even annoying. It is best to find out early if you have the temperament and lifestyle to appreciate the Min Pin's temperament and lifestyle, because the Min Pin is not going to change.

In many ways the Miniature Pinscher resembles a tiny deer.

Min Pins are self-appointed guardians of the home turf.

Differences in breeds: Far too often, dogs are acquired with the idea that all breeds act the same. They don't. The very reason that different breeds were initially created stemmed from dif-

Stag red Min Pins have black hairs interspersed among the red.

The Min Pin at a Glance

Energy Level:	■■■■■
Exercise requirements:	■■
Playfulness:	■■■■■
Affection Level:	■■■
Friendliness toward Dogs:	■■
Friendliness toward Other Pets:	■
Friendliness toward Strangers:	■
Ease of Training:	■
Watchdog Ability:	■■■■■
Protection Ability:	■
Grooming Requirements:	■
Cold Tolerance:	■
Heat Tolerance:	■■■

ferences in behavior, not looks. Dogs were selected for their propensity to trail, point, retrieve, herd, protect, or even cuddle, with physical attributes often secondary to behavioral. Min Pins are from stock created to seek and destroy rats, a task that required vigilance, courage, and tenacity. Don't get a Miniature Pinscher and ask it to act like a Collie, Retriever, or even a full-size Doberman. It's just not in his genes.

Behavior: So what is in the Min Pin's genes? First of all, recall that Miniature Pinschers are *not* miniature Doberman Pinschers. Despite their appearance, they were not bred down from the larger breed. They are related, and they do share some temperament features, but they differ in as many ways as they are similar. There are individual differences, but the typical Min Pin is an ultralively, bold, inquisitive, energetic, bright, comical, quick-witted dog, full of self-confidence and pride, and always on the lookout for trouble!

Min Pins respond to affection, but are not overly demonstrative; they tend to attach themselves to one member of the family to the exclusion of others. Often, Min Pins not only consider themselves to be a part of the family, but they will try to be the head of it! These little Napoleons do sometimes have a problem in accepting a human as their leader, and dominance struggles are a reported problem.

The Min Pin is a big dog in a little body. If the good manners that are expected of big dogs are also expected of this little big dog, then he can be a well-mannered family member. A spoiled Min Pin is apt to become the family tyrant, so he requires a firm (but gentle) hand and some obedience training. Often headstrong, his diminutive size, nonetheless, makes any harsh corrections inadvisable.

Black and tan Miniature Pinschers may look like miniature Doberman Pinschers, but the Min Pin is actually the older of the two breeds.

Min Pins are excellent watchdogs, and although they will try to be a formidable protection dog, their size makes them more intimidating than effective. Excessive barking can be a problem. They are not very sociable with strangers, and moderately sociable with children. They do like to play, however, and can make an excellent and lively playmate for a gentle child. They may be scrappy with strange dogs, but most can live peacefully with other dogs and pets in the household as long as there is a clear dominance hierarchy.

Playing: Min Pins love to play, and provide their families with hours of entertainment. One need only watch a Min Pin of any age at play with his cache of toys to realize that perhaps the real reason he has been nicknamed the "king of toys" is that surely no dog enjoys toys as much as a Min Pin!

Challenges: In a survey of Miniature Pinscher owners, barking, running away, dominance struggles, guarding of food or objects from family members, and snapping were considered the most common behavior problems.

Blue and tan Min Pins occur when there are two recessive "d" genes. This occurrence causes black pigment to turn gray.

short jogs), protection dog, constant cuddler, fawning admirer, or snap-to-it Lassie clone, you may wish to explore some other breeds than the Min Pin. If your household is made up of a throng of unruly children or large dogs, ask yourself if a small dog would be safe from accidents.

Who should have a Min Pin? Ideal Min Pin owners are patient, gentle, and firm, and with a very good sense of humor. They want a lively dog that will enliven their lives. They don't want a dog as an inanimate ornament, or an automated robot; they want a quick-witted, free-spirited, graceful clown with which they can truly share their lives on a nearly equal partnership, rather than master-servant, basis.

One of a Kind

Many breeds can be described as "acting sort of like a such and such"; the Min Pin is one-of-a-kind. Their owners like it that way. Make every effort to get to know some Min Pins at their homes; you may very well decide that a Min Pin is what your home is lacking.

Upkeep

The Miniature Pinscher is in many ways the toy dog for people who don't usually care for toy dogs. There is nothing "sissy" about this breed, either in appearance, demeanor, or hardiness. Still, no matter how big these dogs consider themselves, they are little dogs and can get hurt by big things. The Min Pin's small bones are extremely dense and strong for their size, but they still are relatively delicate. Added

Some breeders do not advise first-time dog owners to get a Min Pin. Others advocate that Min Pins can make excellent pets, even for a first-time dog owner as long as you take the time to train and socialize your dog, and are educated about the idiosyncrasies of this cocky little dog.

Who should not have a Min Pin? If a primary requirement of your prospective dog is that he be a jogging companion (unless you plan very to the reckless devil-may-care personality so very typical of the Min Pin, the only wonder is that more broken bones are not seen. They are not the breed for a household full of rambunctious children or careless adults. A minor accident for a large dog could prove to be a major accident for a dog this size. An attack from a large dog could prove fatal, so the Min Pin must always be watched when outside of a fenced area, especially because he is likely to be the one that initiates a fracas!

✔ There are many advantages to being small; a small food bill is one of them. Almost everything costs less for small dogs, including boarding, bathing, shipping, housing, and even clothing. Best of all, they fit in your sports car, your apartment, your bed, and your lap!

✔ The Min Pin is a fastidiously clean breed, with little doggy odor. He seldom requires bathing, and needs only a weekly brushing. His small size and short coat make shedding a minimal problem.

✔ Min Pins demand a soft bed and many creature comforts. They do not like cold weather and cannot be expected to live outdoors.

✔ Although of an independent nature, these dogs will not be happy removed from the hustle and bustle of your family life.

✔ The Min Pin loves to move! He requires plenty of exercise but is capable of getting it in a small area, even if it's in your living room when you are trying to concentrate on other matters.

✔ Although not physically suited to marathon running, he will happily join you for a short jog, a game of fetch, or a roundup of unsuspecting squirrels.

✔ Min Pins must be provided with toys lest their boundless energy lead them into mischief.

Chocolate and tan Min Pins occur when there are two recessive "b" genes. This occurrence causes black pigment to turn brown. These Min Pins have a liver colored nose and amber eyes.

Health and Longevity

Any dog that moves as much as a Min Pin had better be healthy. In fact, Min Pins are an extremely hardy breed, with no particularly prevalent health problems. They commonly live to be about 12 years of age, with many individuals enjoying life well into their teens. Although they do slow considerably with time, they typically enjoy good health even into old age.

Purebred dogs are often beset by hereditary health problems that are more prevalent in particular breeds. The best-documented of these problems are those involving joints and eyes.

Predicting Coat Color

Min Pins can vary in both their pattern of coloration or in their shade of coloring, and several different genes are involved in determining what the final product will be. The genetics are not as clear-cut as in some breeds, but the following model works in most cases:

Min Pins come in two basic patterns: self-colored—meaning basically the same color all over—such as red or stag red, and tan-pointed, as in the black and tan. These are controlled by genes at the A-locus:

✔ A^s: Self-colored; dominant, so that self-colored dogs can have either the gene pair A^s/A^s or A^s/a^t.

✔ a^t: Tan-pointed; recessive, so that tan-pointed dogs must have the gene pair a^t/a^t.

The above is the typical way these genes act in most breeds, but the situation is not so clear-cut in Min Pins. For example, there are reports that two red dogs bred together can produce both reds and black and tans, and two black and tans bred together can produce both reds and black and tans. This is probably because of the additional interaction with the genes at another location, the **E** genes. These genes also determine whether a dog is red or stag red.

✔ **E**: Allows black hairs to form. A stag red (or a black and tan) needs at least one copy of E (E/E or E/e).

✔ **e**: Does not allow black hair to form. Clear reds must have two copies (e/e).

This means that stag red, clear red, and tan pointed dogs can be produced from all combinations of parental colors with the following exceptions:

✔ Clear red bred to clear red should result only in clear red offspring.

✔ Tan-pointed bred to tan-pointed should result in only tan-pointed and clear red offspring.

A tan-pointed dog can be black and tan, chocolate and tan, or blue and tan. These colors are controlled by genes at two other locations:

Gray versus black is determined by the **D** gene:

✔ **D**: Causes any black hair to be intensely pigmented, or black. Dominant, so that dogs with black hairs can be either **D/D** or **D/d**.

✔ **d**: Causes any black hair to be diluted, or grayish. The resultant color is called "blue." Recessive, so that any blue dogs are **d/d**.

Brown versus black is determined by the **B** gene:

✔ **B**: Causes any black hair to be black. Dominant, so that dogs with black hairs can be either **B/B** or **B/b**.

✔ **b**: Causes any black hair to be brown, liver, or "chocolate." Recessive, so that any chocolate dogs are **b/b**. Such dogs also have brown rather than black noses, and light-colored eyes.

The fun starts when you begin to predict colors while keeping in mind the interactions between the patterns and colors. What happens if a dog has the genotype a^t/a^t E/E d/d b/b? All of the areas that are usually black will be diluted by both **b** and **d**, and the result will be a fawn individual, the color referred to in Doberman Pinschers as "Isabella." This color is virtually unseen in Min Pins, because the **b** gene is rare and the **d** gene is rarer, but it is possible.

The show pose is four square, legs perpendicular to the ground, head up, ears up, tail slightly up.

Skeletal ailments: In Min Pins the most common skeletal ailment is Legg-Perthes (or Calve-Perthes) disease (aseptic femoral head necrosis), evidenced by limping in older puppies. Surgery or immobilization may be required. This is a relatively common problem of small breeds, and is in some ways the small breed analog of hip dysplasia, which is more common in large breeds. (Hip dysplasia has been reported in Min Pins, but is rare.) Both conditions affect the hip joint, but Legg-Perthes involves degeneration of the head of the femur bone, and usually affects only one leg. Preliminary data indicate that Legg-Perthes disease may be recessively inherited.

Another common problem of small breeds is patellar luxation, where the kneecap does not properly fit into the groove that should hold it into place. As a result, it sometimes pops out of place, causing the dog to hold its leg up until it

pops back in. This, too, is seen in Min Pins, but not with the frequency as in some other small breeds.

Eye problems: A common visual problem in many breeds is progressive retinal atrophy (PRA); it, too, has been reported in the Min Pin, but is not common. PRA begins as night blindness in the adult dog, gradually resulting in total blindness. Veterinary ophthalmologists can diagnose the disorder in young puppies before any problems would be noticed by the owner. The condition is inherited as a simple recessive trait.

Hernias: Inguinal hernias are not uncommon. Although they are thought to have a hereditary component, the mode of transmission is complex and not understood at present.

Skin problems: The breed is prone to a variety of skin problems, including demodectic mange, but perhaps no more than any other breed. Skin problems are in general the number

The Harlequin

In the early years of the Min Pin's history in America, another coat color pattern was exhibited along with the ones still shown today. The harlequin pattern refers to a pattern consisting of ragged blotches of diluted color interspersed among full color.

Because harlequin Min Pins no longer exist, it's not possible to say with confidence if the pattern was caused by the merle gene, although it would appear to be. Merle acts on either black or brown to produce either blue or red diluted areas; however, it does not affect the tan on tan pointed dogs. It may affect the iris color of the eye, so merles often have blue or partially blue eyes. It takes only one copy of the dominant M allele to create a merle dog. If a dog has two copies of the M allele, it tends to have patches of white, and more importantly, visual and auditory problems. In Min Pins, harlequins were thought to have coat problems.

Harlequins fell out of favor and in the 1950s the pattern became a disqualification. During the next decade or two they are thought to have become extinct. The European FCI maintains a separate registry for them as Harlekinpinschers, but none has been registered with them since World War II.

red (which may be an even lighter red as a puppy). Black and rust Min Pins have the same basic color pattern that is seen on Doberman Pinschers or Manchester Terriers. Less common are the chocolate Min Pins, with the same markings as the black and rust but in a dilute brown tone. These dogs usually have amber-colored eyes and brown noses. The genetics of these coat colors are outlined on page 12. Min Pins also come in "blue," which is a light gray version of the black and rust. These dogs are not allowed to be shown. Rarely, fawn Min Pins occur, but these, too, are not showable. The blues and fawns may have some hair and skin problems, but this has not been convincingly documented.

In all colors, the presence of white spots over 0.5 inch (1.3 cm) in diameter or a patch of black hair surrounded by rust ("thumb marks") on the front of either front ankle is not acceptable for show potential Min Pins.

All Min Pins Are Not Created Equal

Although at first glance most Min Pins may look alike, to the experienced eye there are dramatic differences between individuals. The standard of perfection for the breed does not cover every detail and is open to interpretation in several areas. Not all breeders agree on just how refined a Min Pin should be, or just how high they should prance, or any of a number of

one complaint of all dog breeds treated by veterinarians. The "blues" may have a tendency to have hair loss problems.

Color Choices

The most popular colors are the reds, either a deep rich mahogany "stag red" (which are often born almost black, and gradually lose most of the black hairs with maturity), or a bright clear

Chocolate

Chocolate Min Pins were allowed to be shown in most European countries until recently, when the FCI classification scheme dropped them from the list of allowable colors.

other variable traits. No dog is perfect, so some breeders may emphasize perfect showmanship, whereas others perfect proportions, and others perfect movement. As you see more Min Pins from different lineages, these differences will become more apparent to you, and you may begin to form an opinion as to which traits are most important to you. The more subtle differences will probably matter to you only if you wish to acquire a show-quality dog.

Those Irresistible Ears

Part of the appeal of the Miniature Pinscher is its alert, intelligent expression, which is in part due to its characteristic cropped ears. Cropping is not mandated for show-quality Min Pins, but most show dogs do have cropped ears and although it shouldn't matter in judging, there is a perception that uncropped dogs are at a disadvantage in the show ring. Uncropped ears give the dog a softer, less keen expression. They are longer, more rounded, and especially, wider at the base. Many times they will not stand up, so that cropping is necessary to avoid a flop ear. Hanging ears do not predispose the dog to ear problems, or is sometimes argued. There are breeders specializing in freestanding uncropped ears, however, and most uncropped ears can be encouraged to stand by taping them during critical growth phases.

Cropping requires surgery under general anesthesia at about 12 weeks of age. It involves cutting away the outer section of the ear from top to bottom, suturing the cut surface, adhering the ears to a little "dunce cap" for two to three weeks postoperatively, and then taping them for support for some time longer (varying with individuals). The procedure is somewhat painful for

the puppy and if you are definitely not interested in showing, you may not wish to subject your new dog and yourself to this process.

Some people consider cropping cruel and it is against the law in some countries. Some veterinarians are choosing not to crop ears for humane reasons. Speak to your dog's breeder about your desires, and make sure you are in agreement before you buy a puppy.

IN SEARCH OF THE PERFECT MIN PIN

Min Pins have pranced their way into hearts and homes of people around the world. But how to find the perfect Pinscher puppy for you?

Whether you want pet-, show-, or breeding-quality, you must be very careful about where you find your Min Pin. You want to avoid puppies from parents whose only claim to breeding quality is fertility. And you want to avoid buying from a breeder whose only claim to that title is owning a fertile Min Pin.

Good Breeders

Even though you simply want a companion, it's in your best interest to buy from a responsible breeder who breeds for quality Min Pins. Such breeders usually have companion-quality dogs that look just as beautiful, have just as good personalities, are just as healthy, and have been raised with the same love and care as their

Many people contend that uncropped Min Pins have a special appeal because they have more expressive ears.

next Best in Show prospect. You won't find these breeders through pet shops or classified ads or Internet puppy sources—responsible Min Pin breeders sell puppies only to people they have met and interviewed. They want their buyers to go through some effort to find them. They've put a lot of work into their puppies, and they expect you will be willing to put a lot of effort into the one puppy you hope to take home.

Where to look: Finding a responsible Min Pin breeder requires only that you know where to look. The Miniature Pinscher Club of America maintains a breeder referral of MPCA members at *www.minpin.org/breed_dir.htm*. You can also find dedicated breeders in magazines such as *Top Notch Toys* magazine. All-breed magazines, such as *Dog World*, may also be a source of reputable breeders.

Criteria: No matter how you find them, the breeders of your prospective Min Pin puppy

While choosing a new friend is no simple task, it is one of the most rewarding tasks you'll ever undertake.

should all meet the following criteria. They should

✔ breed only one or two breeds of dogs, so they can concentrate on just those breeds.

✔ breed no more than three or four litters per year, so they can concentrate on those litters.

✔ be able to compare their dogs objectively to the Miniature Pinscher standard.

✔ be able to discuss Miniature Pinscher health concerns and provide evidence of the health of their own dogs.

✔ be able to give substantial reasons relating to quality of conformation, temperament, and health why they bred the litter or chose those parents.

✔ have pictures of several generations of the puppy's ancestors.

✔ have clean, friendly, healthy adults.

✔ have clean facilities that promote interaction with their dogs.

✔ raise their litter inside the house and underfoot, not in a kennel or garage.

✔ question you about your facilities, your prior experiences with dogs, and your intentions regarding your new dog.

✔ sell companion-quality puppies only if they are neutered or spayed, or with AKC limited registration, which means their progeny cannot be registered.

✔ insist upon taking the dog back should you be unable to keep her at any time during her life.

Avoid breeders who raise their puppies only on wire-floored pens or in places where they cannot go outside to relieve themselves. Puppies begin to form potty habits at around five weeks of age. If they become used to soiling inside, even at that early age, it becomes ingrained and more difficult to change at a later age. You want a breeder who raises the puppies where they have access to an outdoor potty area. Equally important is access to people and stimulation. The age before 12 weeks of age is the easiest time for a puppy to accept new things in her life, and the best time to make sure the puppy is exposed to as many good experiences with new things as possible.

Many Min Pin breeders insist upon keeping their puppies until 12 weeks of age, which is older than breeders of larger dogs do. Consider this a good sign. Toy dogs are subject to hypoglycemia and unless you're experienced with them, they may be safer with the breeder.

Health Clearances

Good breeders place health at the top of their list. They are familiar with Min Pin health concerns and willing to talk about the health histories of their dogs. They screen their dogs for Min Pin health problems and provide these clearances to you when you look at the litter. With Min Pins, ask about the following:

Legg-Calvé-Perthes disease: The Orthopedic Foundation for Animals maintains a listing of Min Pins screened for this on their web site at *www.offa.org*. It requires the breeder to submit radiographs taken by a veterinarian of the dog's hips.

Mucopolysacharidosis VI: A DNA test is available that can determine if a dog is affected, a carrier, or normal. Although the optimal situation is to breed only normals to normals, it's nonetheless safe to breed a carrier or an affected dog to a normal, as the disease is a recessive and the goal is to avoid producing affecteds.

Patellar luxation: The Orthopedic Foundation for Animals also maintains a registry for this condition that affects the knee.

Eye conditions: Min Pins, like most breeds, can be subject to various eye conditions. Some reports of progressive retinal atrophy exist, and corneal dystrophy also occurs. A veterinary ophthalmologist can send a report so a cleared dog can be registered with the Canine Eye Registration Foundation (*www.vmdb.org/history.html*). The clearance is good for only one year, though, as eye problems can crop up at any time in a dog's life.

The best way to predict how your puppy will look and act is to look to the dam.

Heart conditions: Like any dog, Min Pins can suffer from heart problems. The Orthopedic Foundation for Animals also maintains a registry for cardiac clearances.

Note: Chances are that even good breeders will not have all these clearances for their stock. The eye clearances are simple, but eye problems are not that widespread. The cardiac clearances are usually expensive, and because heart problems aren't that common, most Min Pin breeders forego them. Sometimes, breeders will just use a report from a local veterinarian, especially for patellar luxation. If the parents are not both cleared using DNA for mucopolysacharidosis, you can ask to have your prospective puppy tested to make sure she is clear.

To Pick a Min Pin Puppy

As you finally look upon this family of canine jumping beans, you may suddenly find it very difficult to be objective. How will you ever decide? If you want a show puppy, let the breeder decide. In fact, the breeder knows the puppies' personalities better than you will in the short time you can evaluate them, so listen carefully to any suggestions the breeder has, even for a pet. It is human nature to pick "extremes," but most breeders would advise against choosing either the boldest Min Pin puppy or any puppy that acts shy. But first decide if this is the litter for you.

TIP

Rescue

There's one situation in which you can forego demanding the requirements of finding a responsible breeder; that's when you elect to adopt a Min Pin in need. Min Pins find themselves in rescue situations for a variety of reasons: Some have been lost, and efforts to find their previous owners were unsuccessful; others have been relinquished to a shelter or rescue, perhaps because the owners were moving, expecting a new baby, or found that owning a dog was more work than they expected.

Whatever the reason, these dogs are filled with love but have no one on whom to lavish it. Occasionally, they have behavior problems, often stemming from poor training or socialization, but good rescue organizations will make sure you know any problems ahead of time and will help you guide your Min Pin to becoming the best dog she can be. Rescue Min Pins range from puppies to seniors, but have in common a need for a forever home they can call their own.

You can search for a Min Pin in need through MPCA Rescue (*www.minpin.org/ rescue.htm*), the Internet Miniature Pinscher Service (IMPS; www.minpinrescue.org), or through www.petfinder.com (see page 92 for additional contact information).

Hold a puppy firmly and securely so that she cannot be dropped or unexpectedly squirm out of your arms.

A puppy from parents and pedigree cleared for hereditary health problems has a better chance of being clear herself of such problems.

"Pick me! No, pick me!" All else being equal, you should choose the puppy that is middle of the road, neither the largest nor smallest, most confident nor most shy.

Appearance: By eight weeks of age, baby Min Pins should look like miniature adults. Of course, they will look comparatively stockier and uncoordinated, and their ears may not yet be fully erect, but they should generally be recognizable as Miniature Pinschers. Dark nose pigmentation, absent at birth, should be present by this age. The tail should be docked, and usually the dewclaws. The ears will not be cropped until 12 weeks of age. Ears that are not standing by 12 weeks of age will probably never stand unless they are cropped. In an unpublished study of 50 Min Pin puppies, those that were between 6¼ inches to 8 inches (15–20 cm) at age 8 weeks, or 7½ inches to 9½ inches (19–24 cm) at 12 weeks, grew to be of proper height as adults. Note that all measurements are made of height at withers.

Normal Min Pin puppies are friendly, curious, and attentive. If they are apathetic or sleeping, it could be because they have just eaten, but it could also be because they are sickly.

• The puppies should be clean, with no missing hair, crusted or reddened skin, or signs of parasites.

• Eyes, ears, and nose should be free of discharge. Examine the eyelids if such a discharge is present to ensure that it is not due to the lids or lashes rolling in on the eye and causing irritation.

Everybody needs a new best friend.

• The teeth should be straight and meet up evenly, with the top incisors just overlapping the lower incisors.
• The gums should be pink; pale gums may indicate anemia.
• The area around the anus should have no hint of irritation or recent diarrhea.
• Puppies should not be thin or excessively potbellied.
• The belly should have no large bumps indicating a hernia.
• By the age of 12 weeks, male puppies should have both testicles descended in the scrotum.

If the puppy of your choice is limping, or exhibits any of the above traits, express your concern and ask to either come back the next week to see if she has improved, or to have your veterinarian examine her. In fact, any puppy you buy should be done so with the stipulation that she is pending a health check (at your expense) by your veterinarian.

Medical history: The breeder should furnish you with a complete medical history including dates of vaccinations and worming. If the puppies' ears have not been cropped, discuss the pros and cons of this procedure with the breeder before leaving with your puppy. Veterinarians differ in their cropping skill, and your breeder may wish to suggest a veterinarian with Min Pin cropping expertise. If the ears have already been cropped, be sure you understand any special care you must give them.

You may still find it nearly impossible to decide which whirling dervish will be yours. Don't worry—no matter which one you choose, she will be the best one. In years to come, you will wonder how you were so lucky to have picked the marvel Min Pin of the millennium; you must realize that your Min Pin will be wonderful, in part because you are going to make her that way!

RAISING YOUR MINIATURE PINSCHER

Are you ready for a ricocheting Min Pin bullet? Get ready now, before your whirling dervish is underfoot.

Safe Havens

The Min Pin Den

Many new dog owners are initially appalled at the idea of putting their pet in a cage (or crate) as though he were some wild beast. At times, though, your Min Pin puppy can be a wild beast, and a crate is one way to save your home from ruination and yourself from insanity. But a crate can also provide a quiet haven for your Min Pin. Just as you hopefully find peace and security as you sink into your own bed at night, your puppy needs a place that he can call his own, a place he can seek out whenever the need for rest and solitude arises. Used properly, your Min Pin will come to think of its crate not as a way to keep

Whichever puppy you choose, prepare for the friend of a lifetime!

himself in, but as a way to keep others out! Like his wild ancestors, the Min Pin appreciates the security of his own den.

A crate is the canine equivalent of an infant's crib. It is a place for naptime, a place where you can leave your puppy without worry of him hurting himself or your home. It is not a place for punishment, nor is it a storage box for your dog when you're through playing with him.

Place the crate in a corner of a quiet room, but not too far from the rest of the family. Put the puppy in the crate when he begins to fall asleep, and he will become accustomed to using it as his bed. Be sure to place a soft double pad in the bottom. And by taking the puppy directly from the crate to the outdoors upon awakening, the crate will be one of the handiest house-training aids at your disposal.

The Min Pin Pen

An exercise pen (commonly referred to as an "X-pen") also fulfills many of the same functions as a crate. These are transportable wire folding "playpens" for dogs, typically about 4 by 4 feet (1.2 × 1.2 m). In fact, if you must be gone for hours at a time, they are the perfect answer because the puppy can relieve himself on paper in one corner, sleep on a soft bed in the other, and frolic with his toys all over! It's like having a little yard inside—the canine equivalent of the baby's playpen.

Decide now where you intend to keep your new family member. Min Pins are obviously not outdoor dogs, although they will enjoy the opportunity to spend part of their days outside, weather permitting. Your Min Pin will want to be in the thick of things, and participate in everything your family does. So plan for your Min Pin to be quartered in the house where he can be around activity, but not necessarily always underfoot.

It is best that the new puppy not have the run of the entire house. Choose an easily Min Pin-proofed room where you spend a lot of time, preferably one that is close to a door leading outside. Kitchens and dens are usually ideal. When you must leave your dog for some time, you may wish to place him in a crate, X-pen, secure room, or outdoor kennel. Bathrooms have the disadvantage of being so confining and isolated that puppies may become

An X-pen provides an indoor yard and is perfect if you must be gone for long periods.

The Homecoming Kit

✔ Buckle collar (cat collar for puppies): for wearing around the house.

✔ Nylon or fine chain choke collar: safer for walking on leash.

✔ Lightweight leash: nylon, web, or leather—never chain! An adjustable show leash is good for puppies.

✔ Lightweight retractable leash: better for older dogs; be sure not to drop them, as they retract toward the puppy and can frighten him.

✔ Stainless steel flat-bottomed food and water bowls; avoid plastic as it can cause allergic reactions and hold germs.

✔ Crate: just large enough for an adult dog to stand up in without having to lower his head.

✔ Exercise pen: tall enough that an adult dog can't jump over, or preferably with a top.

✔ Toys: latex squeakies, fleece-type toys, balls, stuffed animals stuffed socks. Make sure

squeakies and the eyes of stuffed animals can't be ingested.

✔ Chew bones: the equivalent of a teething ring for babies.

✔ Antichew preparations.

✔ Baby gate(s): better than a shut door for placing parts of your home off limits.

✔ Soft brush.

✔ Nail clippers.

✔ Dog shampoo.

✔ First aid kit.

✔ Sweater: for cold climates.

✔ Food: start with the same food the puppy is currently eating.

✔ Dog bed: a round fleece-lined cat bed is heavenly, but you can also use the bottom of a plastic crate, or any cozy box, padding with two layers of blankets to accommodate a burrowing Min Pin. Wicker will most likely be chewed to shreds, and should be avoided!

✔ Camera and film! (A telephoto lens is a necessity.)

destructive; garages have the disadvantage of also housing many poisonous items.

Min Pin Mishap Prevention

Outside

Fences: If you have a yard, the number one safety item is a secure fence. Min Pins, like all dogs, would love to run loose and rule the neighborhood. But they probably wouldn't live long if they did. Because Min Pins are blissfully ignorant of the dangers that lurk for a little dog in the big outdoors, it is vital that you prevent such roaming. Luckily, Min Pins are not known for their fence-jumping prowess (although they can jump considerably higher than most other dogs their size), but they are adept burrowers and squeezers. A small hole in the fence is all one needs to wriggle his way to freedom. Many dogs are actually inadvertently taught to escape by their owners. Perhaps the new owner has an old fence, and decides to wait and see if it will hold the dog. When the dog squeezes out of the biggest holes, the owner patches those. Then the dog looks for the next biggest hole, and

Check your yard to make sure no poisonous plants are within your puppy's reach.

dog within are no good for Min Pins; they don't keep other animals out. If you live in a rural area, wild animals (including alligators, coyotes, and hawks) may look upon your puppy as a snack. Still, the number one predator of any dog is the automobile. Good fences make live dogs!

Bushes, trees, plants: There can still be dangers within the yard, though. Are there bushes with sharp, broken branches at Min Pin eye level? Are there trees with dead branches in danger of falling, or even heavy falling fruits or pinecones? Are there poisonous plants? (Some of the more deadly are yew, mistletoe, English holly berries, philodendron, Jerusalem cherry, azaleas, rhododendron, foxglove, water hemlock, milkweed, rattlebox, corn cockle, jimsonweed, jessamine, oleander, and castor bean).

Pools: If you have a pool, be aware that although dogs are natural swimmers, a little Min Pin cannot pull himself up a swimming pool wall and can drown.

Inside

Min Pin-proofing your home has two goals: protecting your Min Pin, and protecting your home. The first step is to do everything you would do to babyproof your home. Get down at puppy level and see what dangers beckon.

✔ Puppies love to chew electrical cords in half, and even lick outlets. These can result in severe burns, loss of the jaw and tongue, and death.

✔ Running into a sharp table corner could cause an eye injury.

✔ Jumping up on an unstable object could cause it to come crashing down, perhaps crushing the puppy.

squeezes out of it. Finally, as the fence comes to resemble a patchwork quilt, the dog is squeezing through holes that you would swear couldn't possibly accommodate a dog with bones. Yet, had the fence only had such tiny holes in the first place, the dog would never have learned to go through them. If you wanted your Min Pin to learn to squeeze through small passages, wouldn't you do so a little at a time? Then why use the same tactic to teach your dog not to squeeze through? If you want your dog to stay in the yard, make the yard Min Pin-proof from the very beginning.

Your fence must not only be strong enough to keep your dog in, but to keep stray dogs out. This is why the "invisible fences" that keep your

There's another reason Min Pins are called the King of Toys: they crave toys!

✔ Do not allow the puppy near the edges of high decks, balconies, or staircases.

Doors: Doors can be a hidden danger area. Everyone in your family must be made to understand the danger of slamming a door, which could catch a Min Pin and break a leg—or worse. Use doorstops to ensure that the wind does not blow doors suddenly shut, or that the puppy does not go behind the door or play. This can be a danger, because the gap on the hinged side of the door can catch and break a little Min Pin leg if the door is closed.

Be especially cautious with swinging doors; a puppy may try to push one open, become caught, try to back out, and strangle. The puppy may not see clear glass doors and could be injured running into them. Never close a garage door with a Min Pin running around. Finally, doors leading to unfenced outdoor areas should be kept securely shut. A screen door is a vital safety feature; Min Pins are adept at sneaking between your legs to freedom when you open the front door.

Household Min Pin Killers

- Rodent baits
- Household cleaners
- Toilet fresheners
- Leaked antifreeze
- Drugs
- Some houseplants
- Chocolate (especially baker's chocolate)
- Nuts, bolts, and pennies
- Pins and needles
- Bones
- Loose toy parts

First Lessons

Off-limits Training

You should have decided before your puppy came home what parts of your home will be off limits. Make sure that every family member understands the rules, and that they understand that sneaking the puppy onto off-limit furniture, for example, is not doing the puppy any favor at all. Your puppy will naturally want to explore everywhere you let him, including climbing on furniture. If you don't want your dog on furniture, a harsh "*No!*" and firm but gentle push away from the furniture should let him realize that this is not rewarding behavior. Don't fling the puppy off of furniture, or use mousetraps on furniture surfaces, because both practices are

Get ready for chaos!

dangerous and absolutely a bad idea unless you like emergency visits to the veterinarian. There are several more humane items (available through pet catalogs) that emit a loud tone when a dog jumps on furniture, but these should not be necessary if you train your young puppy gently and consistently from the beginning.

House-training

All canines have a natural desire to avoid soiling their denning area. As soon as young wolves are able to walk, they will teeter out of their den to relieve themselves away from their bedding. Because you are using a crate for your puppy's den, your Min Pin will naturally try to avoid soiling it. But puppies have very weak control over their bowels, so that if you don't take them to their elimination area often, they may not be able to avoid soiling. Further, if the crate is too large for the puppy, he may simply step away from the area he sleeps in and relieve himself at the other end of the crate. An overly large crate can be divided with a secure barrier until the puppy is larger or house-trained. Even so, just like the wolf cubs, your puppy may step just outside the door of the crate and eliminate there, because to the puppy, that fulfills the natural requirement of not going in the den. The puppy has failed to realize that he has just soiled *your* den. And the more the puppy soils in a particular spot, the more he is likely to return to that same spot.

Toy dogs and house-training: Toy dogs are notoriously difficult to house-train. Some people think it's because their bladders are just so tiny, or that they simply mature later when it comes to urinary sphincter control. Others believe it is a matter of early training. Another theory relates to the size of the puddle a toy

By constantly rotating toys and chew items, your puppy won't get bored with the same ones and will more likely play with them instead of your shoes.

dog creates. A puppy often creates puddles so small nobody notices, and the puppy ends up believing he has acted appropriately. One of the more important theories concerns your puppy's experiences before even coming to you. Many toy breeds are raised indoors in pens. It's easier for breeders to keep them inside where they know they will be safe, rather than try to hustle them outdoors and watch them there. But early habits concerning the proper place to eliminate are formed as early as five weeks of age. A puppy who spends his time indoors is forming a lifelong tendency to consider the indoors appropriate for urinating and defecating.

No matter how hard both of you try, your puppy will almost surely have accidents. If you catch him in the act, pick him up quickly and whisk him outside. If you don't see him doing it, there's nothing you can do. The puppy was not being sneaky or spiteful, and he will have no idea what your problem is if you start yelling and pointing. Such behavior will only convince him that every once in while, for no apparent reason, you go insane. Rubbing his nose in the mess will simply further convince him of your perverse nature.

Carpet cleaning: Puppy owners learn the secrets of carpet cleaning fast. Pick and soak up

CHECKLIST

Accidents

✔ Learn to predict when your puppy will have to relieve himself. Immediately after awakening, and soon after heavy drinking or playing, your puppy will urinate.

✔ You will probably have to carry a younger puppy outside to get him to the elimination area on time.

✔ Right after eating, or if nervous, your puppy will have to defecate. Circling, whining, sniffing, and generally acting worried usually signals that defecation is imminent.

✔ A rule of thumb is that a puppy can hold himself for as many hours as the puppy is months old; that means a two-month-old can wait for two hours, or a four-month-old for four hours, up to about six months old.

✔ Always take the puppy out before his regularly scheduled program of elimination.

✔ Don't just hustle your puppy outside and shut the door. Go with him, and praise him and even give him a treat for relieving himself in the proper place.

Baby gates can keep your Min Pin—and your house—safe. Just be sure the toys are on the same side as the puppy!

as much of the deposit as possible, then add a little water and again soak up as much as possible. If you have a rug cleaner that extracts liquid, now is the time to use it. Next apply an enzyme digester-type odor neutralizer (these are products specifically made for dog accidents); use enough to penetrate the pad. Leave it on for a long time, following directions. Cover the area with plastic so it doesn't dry out before the digester can break down the

urine. The final step is to add a nice odor, such as a mixture of lavender oil or vanilla with baking soda, to the area. Let it air out, then vacuum.

Paper-training: If you cannot be with your puppy for an extended period, you may have to paper-train your puppy. Place newspapers on the far side of the room (or X-pen), away from the puppy's bed or water bowl; near a door to the outside is best. Place the puppy on the papers as soon as he starts to relieve himself. A convenient aspect of paper-training is that the concept of using the paper will transfer to wherever you put the paper, so if you later take the paper outside, it can act as a training tool there.

Litterbox-training: You can also litterbox-train your puppy. Place dog litter in a cat box; add some soiled newspaper or something with the scent of urine, and place the puppy in the box when he begins to urinate. Apartment dwellers may find that a box-trained Min Pin is very convenient on rainy days.

Note: No matter how wonderful and smart your Min Pin is, he probably will not have full control over his bowels until he is around six months of age. Meanwhile, set the stage for a perfect house pet, and chin up! It will get better!

Social Lessons

As with children, early lessons last a lifetime. The lessons your Min Pin puppy learns now will shape his actions for years to come. All dogs begin life relatively fearless, gradually becoming more cautious beginning at around 12 weeks of age. By exposing your puppy to as much as possible while he's still young, he will learn to accept the same experiences later in life, but more than simple exposure is required; the experience must be low stress and rewarding. You should arrange to have favorable interactions with men, women, children, dogs, cats, traffic, stairs, noises, grooming, leash walking, crates, and alone time. Note, however, that until your puppy is at least 12 weeks old and has had two sets of puppy vaccinations, you should avoid exposing him to strange dogs or places where lots of dogs frequent.

Two puppies can be great friends, but you have to make sure each one gets time alone from the other.

TIP

Introducing New Dogs

When introducing new dogs, it is best if both are taken to a neutral site so that territoriality does not provoke aggression. Two people walking the dogs beside each other as they would on a regular walk is an ideal way for dogs to accept each other.

The best time to introduce cats and dogs is when they are still kittens and puppies.

Strangers

Be careful how you introduce your puppy to strangers. Children are drawn to cute puppies, so be sure yours isn't mobbed by a crowd of puppy petters. It's best to let your puppy meet children one by one, with both child and puppy on the ground. That way the puppy can't be stepped on or dropped. Children must be taught that puppies can't be handled roughly. Dogs and young children should always be supervised for the well-being of both of them. Other dogs and babies should also be supervised. Always make a fuss over the dog when the baby is around so the dog will associate the baby with good times.

Being Alone

Don't forget to accustom your puppy to being alone. Dogs are not naturally loners, and being alone is very stressful for them. It must be done gradually, so your puppy knows you're coming back soon. Save special interactive chew toys to occupy the puppy when you are away. Despite your efforts, many dogs will develop separation anxiety (see page 54 for tips on coping with that potentially serious behavioral problem).

Cats

Young Min Pins are more likely to be hurt by a cat than the other way around. An older Min Pin can learn to like cats by introducing them gradually, inside the house. The dog should be held on leash initially, and the cat prevented from running, which would elicit a chase response in the dog. If the dog is fed every time the cat appears, he will come to really appreciate the cat. Many Min Pins have become fast friends with "their" pet cats.

Min Pins can make your yard or even your home into a place of adventure. Otherwise it's seldom safe to let them off lead unless in a fenced area.

How Many Min Pins?

There are certain advantages, and disadvantages, to having more than one dog—two dogs are twice the fun of one, without being twice the work. Consider adding another pet if you are gone for most of the day. Min Pins generally get along well with each other and with other dogs and cats. However, two unneutered males, especially of the same age, are apt to engage in dominance disputes. On the other hand, intact males and females together will provide you with the biyearly problem of keeping Romeo and Juliet separated. Still, Min Pins can make close attachments with their housemates, and will enjoy hours of playing together. In fact, whereas in many ways two dogs are better than one, three dogs are also better than two! With two dogs, a problem can arise when one is left alone while you train or give personal attention to the other. With three, there is always a pair left.

Leash Lessons

Many Min Pins rebel the first time they find themselves at the end of a leash. The old-school way of coping was to simply drag the recalcitrant puppy along until he submitted; the modern way is to make walking on a leash rewarding and fun.

✔ Use a soft collar that won't choke your dog or slip over his head. If he objects to the collar or leash, distract him with treats or even a game until he ignores it.

✔ Have your dog wear it for only a short time and remove it while he's being good.

✔ Repeat several times a day until he associates a collar with good times.

When you attach the leash, don't try to lead your Min Pin anywhere at first; instead, let him proudly lead you around the house and yard. If he appears glued in place, pick him up and move him to another place, or entice him to take a few steps by luring him with a treat. Gradually lure your puppy more and more; require that he take a few steps along with you before he gets the treats . . . then a few more steps. Gradually, he'll figure out that walking alongside you turns you into a human snack dispenser, and he'll be eager to strut alongside.

Min Pin Beginnings

You won't have a second chance to give your puppy a good start on a healthy life. Your veterinarian is your best source of individualized health care, but you should be aware of the basics.

Puppy Food

Feed a high-quality food made especially for puppies. Min Pin puppies don't eat much, so you can afford to buy a more expensive puppy food. Feed your young Min Pin puppy every four hours. From about four to six months of

age, you can feed him either three or four times a day, from six to nine months of age, three times a day, and then gradually cut down to twice a day by the time the dog is 12 months old. It's better to feed a Min Pin puppy too often than too seldom, even if it means feeding smaller meals.

Hypoglycemia

Feeding a small-breed puppy entails some special considerations because of the possibility of hypoglycemia, a disorder of the central nervous system caused by low blood sugar. Very small dogs, especially puppies, aren't able to store enough readily available glucose, so when their glycogen (the form in which the body stores glucose) is depleted, their body begins to break down fat for energy. Because small puppies have little fat, that energy source is quickly depleted. When that happens, the brain, which depends on glucose-derived energy to function, starts to function improperly. The dog becomes sleepy, weak, uncoordinated, and loses his appetite. Left untreated, the dog can have seizures, lose consciousness, and die.

This is why it's extremely important to feed young Min Pins lots of small meals—and even more frequently during times of stress or high activity. Meals should be fairly high in protein, fat, and complex carbohydrates. Complex carbohydrates break down more slowly than simple carbohydrates, leading to more efficient use and less likelihood of causing a roller coaster effect of high and low glucose levels.

It's important to feed toy breed puppies often in order to avoid the possibility of hypoglycemia.

Simple carbohydrates: Feed simple carbohydrates immediately if your dog is already showing signs of hypoglycemia, however, as these will be more quickly available to the dog's body as energy. Simple carbohydrates include syrup and several veterinary products such as Nutrical. If your dog can't eat, rub the syrup on his gums; don't try to make him swallow if he may be unconscious. Keep the dog warm, call your veterinarian, and then take him to your veterinarian for treatment, possibly with intravenous glucose. After the dog has recovered, feed him a small, high-protein meal.

Hypoglycemia is mostly a problem of puppies, perhaps related to immaturity of liver cells. Most Min Pins will outgrow it by the time they reach seven months of age. But all Min Pin owners should be aware of the possibility, and take special efforts not to allow their dogs to go too long without eating.

Vaccinations

Well-timed vaccinations are extremely important safeguards for your puppy. Your pup received his early immunity through his dam's colostrum during the first few days of nursing. As long as the puppy still has that immunity, any vaccinations you give him won't provide sufficient immunity, but after several weeks that immunity begins to decrease. As his immunity falls, both the chance of a vaccination being effective and the chance of getting a communicable disease rise; the problem is that immunity diminishes at different times in different dogs. So starting at around six weeks of age, a series of vaccinations is given in order to catch the time when they will be effective, while leaving as little unprotected time as possible. During this time of uncertainty it's best not to take your puppy around places where unvaccinated dogs may congregate. Some deadly viruses, such as parvovirus, can remain in the soil for six months after an infected dog has shed virus in his feces there.

Core and noncore vaccines: Vaccinations are divided into core vaccines, which are advisable for all dogs, and noncore vaccines, which are advisable for only some dogs. Core vaccines are those for rabies, distemper, parvovirus, and hepatitis (using the CAV-2 vaccine, not the CAV-1, which can cause adverse reactions and is still sold by some feed stores). Noncore vaccines include those for leptospirosis, corona virus, tracheobronchitis, Lyme disease, and giardia. Your veterinarian can advise you if your dog's lifestyle and environment put the dog at risk for these diseases.

A sample core vaccination protocol for puppies suggests giving a three-injection series at least two weeks apart, with each injection containing distemper (or measles for the first injection), parvovirus, adenovirus 2 (CAV-2), and parainfluenza (CPIV). The series should not end before 12 weeks of age. A booster is given one year later, and are then given every three years. Rabies should be given at 16 weeks of age, with boosters at one- to three-year intervals according to local law.

Some people contend that small dogs, such as Min Pins, should get smaller doses of vaccination; however, veterinarians disagree. The immune system doesn't work based on size; after all, the same amount of virus is sufficient to infect small dogs and large dogs alike.

Note: Some proponents of natural rearing condemn vaccinations and instead use homeopathic nosodes. However, no controlled study has ever supported the effectiveness of nosodes.

The Miniature Pinscher is a sturdy, compact, proud, and alert dog.

Deworming

Your puppy should have been checked and dewormed if necessary before coming home with you. Most puppies have worms at some point because some types of worms lie dormant and protected in the dam until hormonal changes caused by her pregnancy activate them and enable them to infect her puppies. Your puppy can also pick up worms from the ground in places where dogs congregate. The best prevention at home is to clean up feces immediately. Some heartworm preventives also prevent many types of worms. Get your puppy regular fecal checks for worms, but don't deworm your puppy unnecessarily. Avoid over-the-counter worm medications, which are neither as safe nor effective as those available from your veterinarian.

If you see small, flat, white segments in your dog's stool, he may have tapeworms. Tapeworms are acquired when your puppy eats a flea, so the best prevention is flea prevention. Tapeworms require special medication to get rid of them.

Heartworm prevention: Heartworms are carried by mosquitoes, so if there is any chance of a single mosquito biting your Min Pin he needs to be on heartworm preventive medication. Ask your veterinarian when the puppy should begin taking the medication, as it may vary according to your location. Dogs over six months of age should be checked for heartworms with a simple blood test before beginning heartworm prevention. The once-a-month preventive is safe, convenient, and effective. Treatment is available for heartworms, but it's far cheaper, easier, and safer to prevent them. Left untreated, heartworms can kill your dog.

Spaying and Neutering

Most pet owners will find that life with a spayed or neutered dog is much easier than life with an intact one. An intact (unspayed) female comes into estrus twice a year, usually beginning at around eight months of age. Intact females are at increased risk of developing breast cancer and pyometra, a potentially fatal infection of the uterus. Spaying negates the possibility of pyometra, and spaying before the first season significantly reduces the chance of breast cancer.

Intact males are more likely to fight, mark your furniture with urine, and to develop testicular cancer and prostatitis. The major drawbacks are that each procedure requires surgery and anesthesia, that many spayed and neutered dogs gain weight, and that some spayed females develop urinary incontinence (although this is a more common concern in large breeds). Talk to your veterinarian and breeder about the pros and cons.

Docking and Cropping

Tails: Min Pin tails are customarily docked, and dewclaws removed, between one and three days of age. This is not a home project. Too many novice breeders think they can save a buck by cutting off a tail at home, but it requires knowledge of anatomy to do correctly. Done incorrectly, the dog's tails can become infected and have to be totally amputated. If you miss doing it in these early days, it becomes a serious surgery and should not be done at all. Tail docking is a cosmetic procedure; it is not necessary if you do not intend to show your Min Pin. For purposes of selling puppies, however, you may find an undocked dog more difficult to sell. Removal of dewclaws may help prevent torn nails as an adult, and is more widespread among all breeds.

Ears: Cropping is done at around 12 weeks of age. It must be performed only by a veterinarian and under general anesthesia; it's best to find a veterinarian experienced with Min Pin ears. The floppier the ear, the shorter the crop needed to make the ears stand erect. The ears must be subsequently attended to and trained over the next few weeks, requiring cleaning and taping every few days. Many breeders tape a plastic cup on the head and use it as a splint to help guide the ears. Again, cropping is not necessary, not even if you want to show your dog. Both cropping and docking do involve pain, and some countries have banned them. Talk to your veterinarian about your choices before making a decision.

In order to share your life with your Min Pin, you need to realize that he inhabits a very different world than yours. The size difference is self-evident, but differences in the sensory worlds of humans and dogs are not as obvious.

Vision

The canine eye does not see the world with as much detail or color as does the human eye. Dogs can see colors, but their sense of color is like that of a color-blind person. That is, dogs confuse similar shades of yellow-green, yellow, orange, and red, but can see and discriminate blue, indigo, and violet from all other colors and each other as well as humans can. This does not mean the dog's eye is inferior to the human's; it is superior when it comes to seeing in very dim light.

Light passes through the cornea and pupil of the eye and is focused by the lens onto the retina. Min Pins are susceptible to disorders of both the lens and retina, which can impair vision.

Whether with cropped or uncropped ears, the Min Pin has acute hearing. Note that the deep canal makes the dog's ear susceptible to various fungal and bacterial infections.

Olfaction

Your Min Pin has olfactory abilities that are beyond comprehension. It is as though humans are completely blind when it comes to the world of smell, and there is no way one can imagine the vastness of this sensory world that is so very apparent to your dog. The next time you become impatient when your dog wants to sniff something on a walk, consider it the same as when you stop to admire a sunset, much to your Min Pin's bewilderment.

Taste

Dogs also have a well-developed sense of taste, and have most of the same taste receptors that humans do. Research has shown that they prefer meat (not exactly earthshaking news), and although there are many individual differences, the average dog prefers beef, pork, lamb, chicken, and horse meat, in that order.

Hearing

Dogs can hear much higher tones than humans can, and so can be irritated by high hums from your TV or from those ultrasonic flea collars. The Min Pin's prick ears are unencumbered by heavy fur and are ideally suited for detecting and localizing sounds, more so than dogs with other ear configurations.

Pain

Because a dog may not be able to express that he is in pain, you must be alert to changes in your dog's demeanor. A stiff gait, reluctance to get up, irritability, dilated pupils, whining, or limping are all indications that your dog is in pain.

Extreme submission.

THE MIN PIN MIND

Let's play!

Min Pin Body Language

Even the little Miniature Pinscher is a wolf at heart, and you can see him exhibit many of the same behavior patterns as his wild ancestors. Dogs, however, differ from wolves in being perpetual juveniles; they never mature mentally to the same level that wolves do. This is one of the results of domestication, and different breeds differ in the extent of this selected infantilism. Still, with careful observation, you can see the wolf in your house.

Wolves and dogs depend upon facial expressions and body language in social interactions:

✔ A yawn is often a sign of nervousness. Drooling can indicate extreme nervousness.

✔ A wagging tail, a lowered head, and exposed teeth upon greeting is a sign of submission.

✔ The combination of a lowered body, a wagging tail, lowered ears, urination, and perhaps even rolling over is a sign of extreme submission.

✔ The combination of exposed teeth, a high, rigidly held tail, raised hackles, very upright posture, a stiff-legged gait, a direct stare, forward pricked ears, and perhaps lifting the leg to mark a tree indicates very dominant, threatening behavior.

✔ The combination of a wagging tail, front legs and elbows on the ground and rear in the air, with or without vocalizations, is the classic "play-bow" position, and is an invitation for a game. This is the Min Pin's favorite pose!

Failures to Communicate

Sometime we expect too much of our dogs when it comes to understanding us, and that lack of understanding can cause serious problems. Make sure you're not making the following mistakes:

• Looking directly at a dog in the eye. Dogs translate this as a threat.

• Striding right up to a dog to meet him. Dogs translate this as a challenge.

• Bending forward when you call a dog. Dogs tend to be pushed away from you by this.

• Slapping a dog on the back or tousling him on top of the head as a sign of affection. Dogs consider these assertions of your dominance.

• Hugging a dog to make him feel secure. Dogs tend to feel uncomfortable when constrained.

Watch Your Tone

✔ Speaking in a high pitched tone tends to encourage dogs to interact and play. It's non-threatening, but because of that, it's easy to ignore.

✔ Speaking in a low-pitched tone indicates power, aggression, and leadership. Use this tone when you need your dog to take notice or stop doing something.

✔ Speaking in long, drawn-out, quiet monotone commands, such as *"Eaaassy,"* *"Staaaaaaay,"* or *"Doown,"* tends to slow and calm your dog.

✔ Speaking with a low-pitched abrupt sound, such as *"NO!"*, *"Aghht!"*, or *"Stop!"* tends to make your dog stop and take notice of you.

✔ Speaking in a series of short, repeated high-pitched sounds that continue to rise in pitch, such as *"Go, go, go, go, go!"* or *"Here, pup, pup, pup, pup, pup!"* tends to speed your dog up.

THE WELL-MANNERED MIN PIN

Part of the Min Pin's appeal is its independent nature and joy of life. Training him won't break his spirit, but it will allow the two of you to enjoy adventures with less friction— as long as you train your dog with love and logic.

Positive Methods and Lots of Rewards

Min Pins don't take well to being bossed and pushed around. For every forceful action, they will offer an equally forceful reaction. Punishment isn't a good way to teach a dog to do anything. About the only thing it's good for is to teach a dog to do nothing—and if you want a dog that does nothing you should get a stuffed toy dog!

The secret of Min Pin training is to convince your dog that it's fun to do what you want him to do. The way to do that is to use positive methods and lots of rewards. Everyone likes to be paid for a job well done.

No breed sits as gracefully as a Min Pin.

Equipment

In the old days your dog had to wear a choke, or slip, collar for training. That's because training traditionally involved correcting the dog with a quick snap and release. It wasn't supposed to choke the dog, but it was supposed to be startling. With positive methods you can use such a collar, but you're just as well off using a buckle collar. You won't be tugging on it. You will want a 6-foot (2.5-m) leash (not chain!) and maybe a 20-foot (6-m) light line.

You will also need lots of tiny dog treats, so small that your dog can swallow them quickly and not let them ruin his dinner. You may also want a special dog toy that you can offer as a reward.

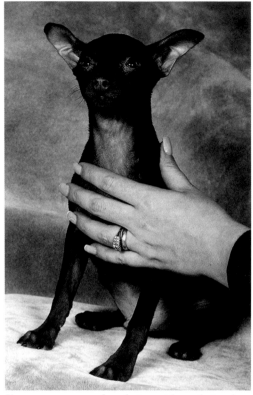

You can use your hands to guide and steady your dog, but not to push and force.

Getting Started

Before you start, find a quiet place away from distractions. Only when your dog learns a skill very well should you gradually start practicing it in other places.

✔ Don't try to train your dog if he's tired, hot, or has just eaten; you want him peppy and hungry for your fun and treats.

✔ Don't train your dog if you're impatient or angry. Losing your cool one time can undo days of proper training.

✔ Keep your training sessions very short; dogs learn best in 10- to 15-minute sessions.

✔ Always quit while your dog is still having fun and doing something he can do well. You can train him several times a day if you want.

Training Like an Expert

There are certain rules that every good trainer should know:

Dog owners are not dog experts: Ignore your well-meaning friends' and neighbors' advice on how to train dogs! Everyone claims to be an authority, but very few people have a clue about the right way to train a dog, yet alone a Min Pin.

Your Min Pin hasn't read the book: Don't be discouraged when things don't go as smoothly as outlined in a book or in a class; they seldom do. Just remember: Be consistent, firm, gentle, realistic, and, most of all, patient.

Be consistent: Sometimes the puppy can be awfully cute when he misbehaves, or sometimes your hands are full, or sometimes you just aren't sure what you want from your Min Pin. But lapses in consistency are ultimately unfair to the dog. If you let the puppy out of his crate because he whines "just this one time," you have taught him that although whining may not always result in freedom, you never know, it just might pay off tonight. In other words, you have taught your puppy to whine.

Say what you mean and mean what you say: Your dog takes his commands literally. If you have taught that "*Down*" means to lie down, then what must the dog think when you yell "*Down*" to make him stop jumping up on you when you return home? If "*Stay*" means not to move until given a release word, and you say "*Stay here*" as you leave the house for work, do you really want your dog to sit by the door all day until you get home?

Think like a dog: In many ways, dogs are like young children; they act to gratify themselves, and they often do so without thinking ahead to consequences. But unlike young children, dogs cannot understand human language (except for those words you teach them), so you cannot explain to them that their actions of five minutes earlier were bad.

Dogs live in the present; if you punish them, they can only assume it is for their behavior at the time of punishment. So if you discover a mess, then drag your dog to it from his nap in the other room, and then scold, the impression to the dog will be that either he is being scolded for napping or that his owner is mentally unstable. Remember, timing is everything in a correction. If you discover your dog in the process of having an "accident," and snatch the dog up and deposit him outside, and then yell "*No*," your dog can only conclude that you have yelled "*No*" to him for eliminating outside. Correct timing would be "*No*," quickly take the dog outside, and then *praise* him once he eliminates outside. In this way you have corrected the dog's undesired behavior and helped the dog understand desired behavior.

Correct and be done with it: Owners sometimes try to make this "a correction the dog will remember" by ignoring the dog for the rest of the day. The dog may indeed remember that his owner ignored him, but he will not remember why. Again, the dog can relate his present behavior only to your actions.

Never rough: Such methods as striking, shaking, choking, and hanging have been touted by some (stupid) trainers: Do not try

A backscratcher and a solid leash guide made from a hollow tube will both help when training your small dog at floor level.

them! They are extremely dangerous, counterproductive, and cruel; they have no place in the training of a beloved family member. Min Pins are a sensitive breed, both mentally and physically, and seldom require anything but the mildest of corrections. A direct stare with a harsh "*No!*" should be all that is required in most cases.

Name, command, action! The first ingredient in any command is your dog's name. You probably spend a good deal of your day talking, with very few words intended as commands for your dog. So, warn your dog that this talk is directed toward him. Many trainers make the mistake of saying the command word at the same time that they are placing the dog into position. This is incorrect. The command comes immediately before the desired action or position. The crux of training is anticipation: The dog comes to anticipate that after hearing a command, he will be induced to perform some action, and he will eventually perform this action without further assistance from you. On the other hand, when the command and action come at the same time, not only does the dog tend to pay more attention to your action of placing him in position, and less attention to the command word, but the command word loses its predictive value for the dog.

Knowing commands to stand, sit, and stay makes portrait taking easy. Or at least, easier. Nothing involving being still is easy with a Min Pin.

Once is enough: Repeating a word over and over, or shouting it louder and louder, never helped anyone, dog or human, understand what is expected of the individual. Your Min Pin is not hard of hearing.

Train before meals: Your puppy will work better if his stomach is not full, and will be more responsive to treats if you use them as rewards. Never try to train a sleepy, tired, or hot Min Pin.

Happy endings: Begin and end each training session with something the dog can do well. And keep sessions short and fun—no longer

---

TIP

Tips for Nips

✔ Never grab at a Min Pin; let him approach you.

✔ Never reach to take a Min Pin out of somebody else's arms.

✔ When handing a Min Pin to someone, hand him to them backwards, so he is facing away from them.

✔ Unlike in humans, where direct eye contact is seen as a sign of sincerity, staring a dog directly in the eye is interpreted by the dog as a threat. It can cause a fearful dog to bite out of what it perceives as self-defense, and is responsible for many dog bites.

Fighting: Cocky Min Pins are sometimes known to challenge strange dogs when good sense should tell them they are overmatched. Keeping your Min Pin on lead and out of reach of other dogs is the best prevention.

More problematic is the case where two dogs that live together do not get along. Dogs may be vying for dominance, and fights will occur until one dog emerges as the clear victor. But even in cases where one dog is dominant, fights may erupt when both are competing for the owner's attention. The dominant dog expects to get that attention before the subordinate, but being a fair-minded owner, one tends to give attention equally, or to even favor the "underdog." This can be interpreted by the dominant dog as an uprising by the subordinate dog, who is then attacked. This is one case where playing favorites (to the dominant dog) will actually be a favor to the subordinate dog in the long run!

It's never too early to train. In fact, young puppies pick up the training concept faster than adults.

than 10 to 15 minutes. Dogs have short attention spans and you will notice that after about 15 minutes, their performance will begin to suffer unless a lot of play is involved. To continue to train a tired or bored dog will result in the training of bad habits, resentment in the dog, and frustration for the trainer. Especially when training a young puppy, or when you have only one or two different exercises to practice, quit while you are ahead! Keep your Min Pin wanting more, and you will have a happy, willing, obedience partner.

Too Much of a Good Thing

There is such a thing as overpraising a dog throughout the day. Think of it this way: if you spend the day praising and petting your Min Pin just for breathing, why should he work for your praise later when he can get it for free? Certainly you should praise, pet, and love your Min Pin, but in some cases of disobedience such "hand-outs" must be curtailed. Such overindulged Min Pins must learn the value of praise by earning it.

Miniature Maneuvering

A big problem when training a little dog is how to guide and correct him. If you bend down to position your Min Pin every time you want him to sit, you will probably have a bad back before you have a sitting dog. Try some of these small dog solutions:

• Teach stationary exercises on a tabletop or other raised surface. This allows you to have eye

Even if you don't need your dog in perfect heel position, you do want your dog to walk nicely at your side without tripping or pulling you.

contact with your dog and gives you a better vantage from which to help your dog learn.

• To train your dog at your feet, extend your arm length with a back scratcher, with which to guide your dog without having to bend over.

• A leash that comes from several feet over-head has virtually no guiding ability whatso-ever. You need a lower pivot point for the leash in relation to the dog, and you can achieve this by what is called a "solid leash." This is simply a hollow, light tube, such as PVC pipe, about 3 feet (91 cm) long, through which you string your leash.

• To prevent a small dog from sitting or lying down, loop part of your regular leash around his belly and hold onto that part, so you have a convenient "handle."

Clicker Training

In order for your Min Pin to make a mental connection between his actions and your rewards, he needs instant feedback; otherwise, if you give him a reward several seconds *after* he has done what you want, he's probably already doing something else and apt to think the later action is what is being rewarded. That means you need to be able to reward him, or at least signal him that he's getting a reward, as soon as you can once he's done something right.

Special sound: Because it's hard to get a treat to your dog instantly, animal trainers use a cue to tell him *"That's right! And your treat is on the way!"* That cue might be a special word, or it could be a special sound the dog doesn't otherwise hear. A special sound is a little more effective because it stands out from the rest of human speech and the dog notices it more readily. Dog trainers use a clicker for this special sound. A clicker is a small device that makes a click sound when pressed with your thumb. They are available from most pet stores. You don't have to use a clicker, but be sure you do use some distinctive sound or word to cue your dog he's on the right track. We will give instructions as though you are using a clicker, but you can substitute another cue.

How to Train with a Clicker

✔ Start by making a click sound and instantly giving your dog a tiny treat. Repeat this many times, until your dog looks expectantly for his treat once he hears the click.

✔ Once he is doing that, you can begin to train your first command, using the clicker. But remem-ber, no dog learns to do something perfectly at first. You have to gradually teach him, shaping his behavior closer and closer to what you want.

✔ Click as he gets warmer, and then gradually require your dog to get a little closer to the final desired action before clicking and treating.

Before beginning, review these clicker basics:
• Give a click instantly when your dog does what you want. The faster you click, the easier it is for your dog to figure out what you like.
• Give a reward as soon as you can after the click.
• Don't forget to praise and pet your dog as part of the reward!
• Always train in gradual steps. Give rewards for getting closer and closer to the final trick.
• Say your dog's name just before you give the command cue word so he knows the next word you say is directed at him.
• Give the command cue just before you get the dog to do the behavior, not during or after it.
• Just say a command cue once, repeating it over and over won't help your dog learn it.
• Once your dog has learned the completed trick and is doing it consistently, you don't have to click your approval every time, but you still need to praise and reward him.

Sit

The traditional way to teach Rocket to sit is to pull up on his collar and push down on his rear while telling him to sit. It works, but it's no fun for either of you. The positive way to train a dog to sit is to use a treat to lure him into a sitting, or near sitting, position. With his rear in a corner so he can't back up, take your treat and hold it just above and behind his nose, so he has to bend his rear legs to look up at it. Click and reward. Repeat several times, then move the treat farther back so your Min Pin has to bend his legs more. Keep on until he has to sit.

Be careful not to smash your little dog into place when teaching the sit.

Once he is sitting reliably to the treat lure, introduce a cue word: *"Rocket, sit."* Gradually fade out use of the treat lure, using just your hand at first, then nothing. Be sure to continue giving it as his final reward, though. Now you are ready to teach some more handy behaviors.

Down

In the old days you would teach Rocket to lie down by wrestling his front legs to the ground. Good luck holding a Min Pin in place! There's an easier way.

Down *must be taught gently or you risk frightening the dog.*

If you first teach your Min Pin to stay on a tabletop when placed there, subsequent lessons can be taught without constantly bending down to Min Pin level.

With your dog sitting or standing, use your treat to lure his nose down and forward. You may have to prevent him from walking forward by gently restraining him with your other hand, or by having him near the edge of a raised surface. Click and reward for just putting his nose down and forward a bit, then for reaching to the ground, then for lowering his elbows a bit, then for lying all the way down. Once he's doing that, click and reward only for doing it when you give the cue: *"Rocket, down!"* Finally, practice on different surfaces.

Stay

Normally, when you teach your dog to *sit* or *down*, he should stay in position until you give a click, which is his release signal. So once your dog knows *sit* or *down*, wait a few seconds after he's in position before clicking and rewarding. Say *"Stay"* (this command doesn't use his name in front of it, because some dogs tend to jump up when they hear their name)

and gradually lengthen the time he must stay before getting the click and reward.

Step out just in front of your dog and stand face to face, then pivot back in place before clicking and rewarding. Gradually step a little farther and farther away, and return to him by circling behind. Go a little farther away, or stay a little longer time, but remember, it's better for him to succeed than to fail, so don't push his limits. If he does get up, simply put him back in position and have him stay a shorter time. Be sure not to stare at him—staring is a threat to dogs and can make a subordinate dog creep to you in submission.

Heel

Your aim in teaching your dog to heel is to have him walk abreast of your left leg. The traditional method to teach a dog to heel was to let him forge ahead and then jerk him back into position. This taught the dog to keep an eye on you because you were an unpredictable menace on a leash. To better watch you, he tended to lag behind you. Heeling was not a happy affair.

Proper heel position keeps the dog out of harm's way as you go about your business.

A kinder, gentler, and more effective way to teach a dog to heel is to reward him for being in the right place at the right time. Place your dog on a leash and just walk with him. Click and reward when he's by your side. Show him a treat and encourage him to walk a few feet with you for it. Click and reward. Work up to slightly longer distances. If he balks or fights the lead, just stop or go in a different direction. You can perfect his position if you want a good heeling dog by rewarding only when he is by your left leg. Again, shape him gradually to get to that point. Once there, introduce the cue: *"Rocket, heel!"*

Many dogs are great backyard heelers but forget all training when they go out in public. Work up to training in places that have more and more distractions and temptations. If Rocket insists on pulling you toward something, turn away from what he wants and ask him to *heel*. Once he does so, click and reward him by saying *"OK"* and then letting him go investigate. Gradually require him to walk a few steps toward the object without pulling before giving him his click and OK.

Come

Your dog already knows how to come when you have something he wants. You need to make sure he knows you have something he wants every time you call. Keep some treats in your pocket, and don't be stingy with them when he comes. Even if he's been up to mischief, be sure not to reprimand your pet when he comes.

If you have a helper, you can play a game that will get your Min Pin puppy really running to you. In an enclosed area, such as a hallway, have your friend hold Rocket while you show him a treat or toy. Back away, enticing him until he's struggling to get to you. Then call out *"Rocket, come!"* and turn and run away from him just as your friend releases him. As he gets to you, click and give him the treat. Make a game out of running faster and farther from him. Always quit while he still wants to play more.

Trick and Treat

The only drawback to teaching basic good manners is that such feats as sitting and staying are not likely to amaze your friends. If you would like to show off your little genius to the neighbors, you'll need a good old-fashioned dog trick. Tricks such as rolling over, playing dead, catching, sitting up, jumping the stick, and speaking are easy to teach using the same training methods as you used for basic obedience. You will find that your particular dog is more apt to perform in ways that make some tricks easier than others to teach. Most Miniature Pinschers are easy to teach to *speak*; wait until it

Calling your puppy with exuberance will help him learn to come quickly and eagerly.

Min Pins love tricks!

The Min Pin Good Citizen

In recent years, there have been an increasing number of laws passed in reaction to the increasing public perception of dogs as ill-mannered, destructive, and dangerous. In an effort to encourage well-mannered, trustworthy dogs, the AKC developed the Canine Good Citizen program, in which such dogs are formally recognized with the Canine Good Citizen (CGC) designation. To pass the CGC test, all your Min Pin must demonstrate is that he will walk quietly with you around other dogs and people; sit for examination; not jump up on, act aggressively toward, or shy from someone who greets you; and stay in place without barking. The CGC is perhaps the most important title that your Min Pin can earn. The most magnificent champion in the show ring is no credit to his breed if he is not a good public citizen in the real world. Every CGC dog promotes goodwill toward dogs when he appears in public. But even if you have no desire to earn a title for your dog, you owe it to yourself, your dog, and your friends to teach your Min Pin these same essential good manners. But before you can teach your Min Pin these essentials, you must teach yourself the essentials of good training techniques.

appears your dog will bark, say "*speak*," and then reward with a treat after the bark. A dog that likes to lie on his back is a natural for *roll over*; give the command when the dog is already on its back, then guide the dog the rest of the way over with a treat. Next start with the dog on his side, then when he is lying on his belly, and finally from a stand. Work gradually to shape the desired final behavior. If your dog can physically do it, you can teach him *when* to do it.

Min Pin Mental Giants

Is your Min Pin "gifted"? Perhaps you and your dog have enjoyed your training sessions and would like to pursue higher education, as well as practice around distractions and discuss problems with people who have similar interests. Most cities have dog clubs or individuals that conduct obedience classes. The AKC or your local Humane Society can direct you to them. You might also contact one of the Miniature Pinscher breed clubs and ask for names of

Regular play sessions can help alleviate destruction due to boredom, but allow the dog time to calm down before leaving. Never get a dog excited and then leave him with only your furniture to play with.

Min Pin obedience enthusiasts in your area. Attend a local obedience trial (contact the AKC for date and location) and ask local owners of happy working dogs (especially Min Pins!) where they train.

Be aware that not all trainers may understand the Min Pin psyche, and not all classes may be right for you and your Min Pin. You may wish to visit a class first without your dog in order to evaluate whether you would be comfortable with their techniques.

The Mightiest Min Pins

If your Min Pin is well behaved and enjoys showing off or meeting new people, you and your dog have a wonderful opportunity to bring joy to others. Studies have shown that pet ownership increases life expectancy and even the simple act of petting animals can lower blood pressure. Yet many of the people who could most benefit from such interaction have no access to pets, either because they can no longer care for a pet or because they are hospitalized. The result is particularly sad for lonely elderly people who may have relied upon the companionship of a pet throughout most of their independent years. Now, nursing home residents and hospitalized children have come to look forward to visits by dogs and other pets. These dogs must be meticulously well mannered and well groomed; to be registered as a Certified Therapy Dog, a dog must demonstrate that

he is obedient and responds to strangers in an outgoing, yet gentle, manner. With his natural spark and joie de vivre, the Miniature Pinscher is bound to liven up any room. Such a little Min Pin would indeed be a giant among dogs.

Dealing with the Misbehaving Min Pin

Min Pins are known mischief makers, and indeed, this is one of the endearing traits of the breed. But often Min Pin bad behavior causes problems for the dog's family or himself, sometimes creating an intolerable situation. Many of these problems can be avoided or cured. But if a problem does arise that you are unable to solve, consult your veterinarian. Some problems have physiological bases that can be treated. Also, your veterinarian may refer you to a specialist in canine behavior problems.

Hyperactivity

Well, what did you expect? Your Min Pin will naturally slow with age, but meanwhile, you will need to cope with his energy level. The best cure for hyperactivity is to exercise your Min Pin's body and mind.
✔ Be sure to schedule play periods and training periods.

✔ An activity such as agility combines mental and physical exercise and can be particularly effective for burning off energy.

✔ Rotate toys every few days before your puppy gets tired of the same old ones.

✔ Be sure to include interactive toys such as those that present your dog with a challenge when he tries to dislodge food from them. These are available at pet stores.

✔ If you absolutely cannot cope with your dog's energy, then ask your breeder for advice or consider finding him a home with an experienced Min Pin owner who appreciates that this is part of being a Min Pin.

Barking

Having a Min Pin doorbell is rather handy, but there is a difference between a dog that will warn you of a suspicious stranger and one that will warn you of a falling leaf. Allow your Min Pin to bark momentarily at strangers, and then call him to you and praise him for quiet behavior, distracting him with an obedience exercise if need be.

Isolated dogs will often bark as a means of getting attention and alleviating loneliness. Even if the attention gained includes punishment, the dog will continue to bark in order to obtain the temporary presence of the owner. The simplest solution is to move the dog's domain to a less isolated location. If this is not possible, the puppy's quiet behavior must be rewarded by the owner's presence, working up to gradually longer and longer periods. The distraction of a special interactive toy, given only at bedtime, may help alleviate barking.

The puppy that must spend the day home alone is a greater challenge. Again, the simplest solution is to change the situation, perhaps by adding another animal—a good excuse to get two Min Pins!

Warning: Min Pins also like to bark when playing!

Digging and Chewing

Many a Min Pin owner has returned home to a scene of carnage, and suspected that some mad dog must have broken into the house and gone berserk; after all, those little Min Pin teeth and paws could never wreak such havoc! Min Pins may be small, but they're quick, and a determined Min Pin can do his share of home destruction when left alone.

The best way to deal with these dogs is to provide both physical interaction (such as chasing a ball) and mental interaction (such as practicing a few simple obedience commands) on a daily basis.

Separation Anxiety

More commonly, destructive behavior in an adult dog is due to separation anxiety. Most owners, upon returning home to such ruination, believe the dog is "spiting" them for leaving him, and punish the dog. Unfortunately, punishment is ineffective because it actually increases the anxiety level of the dog, as he comes to both look forward to and dread his owner's return.

The proper therapy is treatment of the dog's fear of being left alone. This is done by separating the dog for very short periods of time and gradually working to longer periods, taking care to never allow the dog to become anxious during any session. This is complicated when you must leave the dog for long periods during the conditioning program. In these cases, the part of the house in which the dog is left for long periods should be different from the part in which the conditioning sessions take place; the latter location should be the location where you wish to leave the dog after conditioning is completed.

In either case, when you return home, no matter what the condition of the house, greet the dog calmly or even ignore him for a few minutes, to emphasize the point that being left was really no big deal. Then have the dog perform a simple trick or obedience exercise so that you have an excuse to praise him. It takes a lot of patience, and often a whole lot of self-control, but it's not fair to you or your dog to let this situation continue.

House Soiling

There are many reasons why a dog might soil the house. Commonly, the dog was never completely house-trained to start with, and so you must begin house-training anew. Sometimes, a house-trained dog will be forced to soil the house because of a bout of diarrhea, and afterward will continue to soil in the same place. If this happens, restrict that area from the dog, and revert to basic house-training lessons once again.

Submissive Urination

Submissive dogs may urinate upon greeting you; punishment only makes this "submissive urination" worse. For these dogs, keep greetings calm, don't bend over or otherwise dominate the dog, and usually this can be outgrown.

Other Soiling Problems

Some dogs defecate or urinate due to the stress of separation anxiety; you must treat the anxiety to cure the symptom. Older dogs may simply not have the bladder control that they had as youngsters; paper-training or a doggy door is the best solution for them. Older spayed females may "dribble"; ask your veterinarian about estrogen supplementation, which may help. And even younger dogs may have lost control due to an infection. Male dogs may "lift their leg" inside of the house as a means of marking it as theirs. Castration will usually solve this problem; otherwise, diligent deodorizing and the use of some dog-deterring odorants (available at pet stores) may help.

Fearfulness

Despite their generally fearless attitude, Min Pins can develop phobias and other fears. Never push your Min Pin into situations that might overwhelm him. A program of gradual desensitization, with the dog exposed to the frightening person or thing and then rewarded for calm behavior, is time-consuming but the best way to alleviate any fear.

Never coddle your dog when he acts afraid, because it reinforces the behavior. It is always useful if your Min Pin knows a few simple commands; performing these exercises correctly gives you a reason to praise the dog and also increases the dog's sense of security because he knows what is expected of him.

Aggression

Min Pin teeth are not all that miniature, and can inflict considerable damage on human skin. The best cure for aggression is prevention, and the best prevention is to raise your Min Pin with kindness, gentleness, and firmness, not encouraging biting or displays of dominance. Expose the puppy to kind strangers from a young age, and make these interactions pleasurable. Teach your Min Pin to look forward to guests and children by rewarding proper behavior, such as sitting and staying, in their presence, and by having them offer the dog a treat.

MINIATURE PINSCHER NUTRITION

Your Min Pin's health and happiness depend in large part on what you put in her food bowl, yet few topics can cause dog owners such confusion. Understanding some of the basics can help you make the best choices for your dog.

A Weighty Subject

A recent survey of Min Pin breeders listed obesity as a major problem in the breed. It's difficult to believe that these lithe balls of fire couldn't burn off every calorie they ingest, but apparently many Min Pins go about the practice of eating with the same gusto as they attack every other daily adventure. However, as Min Pins grow older, they do slow down, and if their owners continue to feed them the same amounts as they did when younger, then obesity can result. The Min Pin can be demanding, and softhearted owners have difficulty not handing over tasty morsels. But there's also a problem involved when feeding a small dog— little dogs need only a little food, and when

Your Miniature Pinscher is a living monument to the nutrition you provide.

little dogs are given a lot of food they cannot remain little! Because only a little food can be given, whenever table scraps or non-doggy treats are offered, these tidbits leave little room for the balanced diet the dog needs.

Signs

You should be able to just feel the ribs slightly when you run your hands along the rib cage, and there should be a good indication of a waistline, both when viewed from above and from the side. A dog with its backbones or hipbones clearly visible is underweight; one with a dimple at the tail base or a roll of fat over the withers is overweight; one with a shape like a football is obese.

Solution: If your Min Pin is overweight, feed her one of the many low-calorie foods on the market rather than simply feeding her less of a

How much a can a puppy eat? Generally, as much as she wants. But it's better to feed a lot of little meals than a few big ones.

ease, can cause the appearance of obesity and should be ruled out or treated. Even heart disease can lead to the false impression of being overweight.

Underweight

If your Min Pin is underweight, first consult your veterinarian to make sure there isn't a problem. Then try a premium-quality high-calorie dog food available from most major pet food stores. You can also try feeding puppy food; add water, milk, or canned food and heat slightly to increase aroma and palatability. Take care not to reinforce picky eating habits. Some choosy canines are created when their owners begin to spice up their food with especially tasty treats. The dog then refuses to eat unless the preferred treat is offered, and finally learns that if she refuses even that proffered treat, another even tastier enticement will be offered.

Give your Min Pin a good, tasty meal, but don't succumb to Min Pin blackmail or you may be a slave to your dog's gastronomical whims for years to come.

Again, some cases of poor weight are due to problems that your veterinarian must diagnose, for example, internal parasites or kidney disease.

high-calorie food. These foods supply about 15 percent fewer calories per pound. Special care must be taken when putting a small dog on a diet, because she has a high metabolic rate and dissipates heat easily. The Miniature Pinscher cannot store sufficient body fat to endure long periods of food restriction, especially in cold weather. The possibility of hypoglycemia (see page 87) is also a concern. Don't try for overnight results. If your Min Pin remains overweight, make sure family members aren't sneaking it Min Pin munchies! Finally, seek your veterinarian's opinion. Some endocrine disorders, such as hypothyroidism or Cushing's dis-

Food Choices

Commercial dog foods should meet the Association of American Feed Control Officials' (AAFCO) guidelines for a particular age group of dogs. Almost all commercially available foods have a statement on the container certifying that the food meets AAFCO guidelines. Premium dog foods, available from large pet supply chains, usually use better-quality ingredients and exceed AAFCO minimums.

Commercial foods: Commercial foods come in dry, canned, and moist varieties. Dry foods are generally healthiest, provide needed chewing action, are most economical, but tend to be less appealing. Many people mix them with tastier canned foods. Canned foods are usually higher in fat and are tastier. Semimoist foods are high in simple sugar and, although handy for travel, lack the better attributes of the other food types and may not be a good choice for dogs predisposed to hypoglycemia. Dog treats may not always meet AAFCO requirements for a complete diet but are fine as supplements.

Home-prepared foods: Home-prepared diets, which have become increasingly popular, have the advantage of using fresh, human-quality ingredients. If they are prepared according to recipes devised by certified canine nutritionists, they should have the correct proportion of nutrients. Unlike commercial dog foods, such diets are not customarily tested on generations of dogs, which makes them vulnerable to looking healthy on paper but not being properly digested or utilized. They can also be labor-intensive, although large batches can be made and frozen.

Raw foods: BARF (Bones And Raw Food) diets, which are made up of raw meat and fresh vegetables, are also increasingly popular. Although dogs have better resistance to bacterial food poisoning than humans do, such diets have nonetheless occasionally been associated with food poisoning, often from salmonella, in dogs. Commercially available meats

--- TIP ---

Changing Foods

When changing foods you should do so gradually, mixing in progressively more and more of the new food each day for several days.

One of the great mysteries of life is why a species, such as the dog, that is renowned for its lead stomach and preference to eat out of garbage cans, can at the same time develop violently upset stomachs simply from changing from one high-quality dog food to another. But it happens.

may be awash in contaminated liquids. Perhaps the worst problem with the BARF diets, however, is that most people who claim to use them never bother to find a nutritionally balanced diet, but instead rely on friends who advocate a solid diet of chicken wings or some equally unbalanced diet.

Human foods: Table scraps, if fed in excess, can throw off the nutrient balance of a diet; however, a few table scraps can be good for a diet and are certainly appreciated by most Min Pins. After all, *you* don't always eat a perfect diet! But choose your scraps carefully. Avoid hunks of fat, which can bring on pancreatitis.

Dry food is most economical, but the least favorite of dogs.

Unlike their ancestors, modern dogs can't hunt for their food. They depend on you for their entire diet.

TIP

Human Foods

Avoid the following human foods that are toxic to dogs:
- Onions cause a condition in which the red blood cells are destroyed. Eating an entire onion could be fatal.
- Chocolate contains theobromine, which can cause death in dogs.
- Macadamia nuts cause some dogs to get very ill; the cause isn't understood.
- Raisins and grapes have been associated with kidney failure and extreme sudden toxicity in some dogs.

Reading the Label

Dogs are carnivores, but they do not live by meat alone. Their nutritional needs are best met by a diet rich in meat that also contains some vegetable matter. Meat is tastier to dogs, higher in protein, and more digestible (meaning smaller stools and fewer gas problems) than plant-based ingredients. A rule of thumb is that at least three of the first six ingredients of a dog food should be animal-derived. Beyond that, you should know a little bit about nutrition.

Nutrition: A good diet must have balanced levels of protein, fat, carbohydrates, vitamins, minerals, and water. How much of each nutrient should your dog get? It depends. Growing dogs need more protein, active dogs need more protein and fat, fat dogs need more protein and less fat, and sick dogs need reduction or addition of various ingredients according to their illnesses. When comparing commercial food labels, you have to compare their dry matter; otherwise, the higher the moisture content, the lower the nutrients levels appear.

Protein: This provides the building blocks for bone, muscle, coat, and antibodies. Eggs, followed by meats, have higher quality and more digestible proteins than do plant derived proteins.

Fat: Fat provides energy, aids in the transport of vitamins, and adds taste. Too little fat in the diet (less than 5 percent dry matter) results in dry coats and scaly skin. Too much fat can cause

Canned food is tasty, but can be expensive.

The Miniature Pinscher is among the most elegant and lithe of breeds. If your dog loses that trim outline, a diet may be in order.

diarrhea, obesity, and a reduced appetite for more nutritious foods.

Carbohydrates: These abound in plant and grain ingredients. Dogs can't utilize their nutrients from carbohydrates unless the carbohydrates are cooked; even then, they utilize them to different degrees depending on their source. Carbohydrates from rice are best utilized, followed by potato and corn, and then wheat, oat, and beans. Excessive carbohydrates in the diet can cause diarrhea, flatulence, and poor athletic performance.

Vitamins: Vitamins are essential for normal life functions. Dogs require the following vitamins in their diet: A, D, E, B1, B2, B12, niacin, pyridoxine, pantothenic acid, folic acid, and

"Ahem. I'm pretty sure it's feeding time."

choline. Most dog foods have these vitamins added in their optimal percentages, so that supplementing with vitamin tablets is rarely necessary.

Minerals: These help build tissues and organs, and are part of many body fluids and enzymes. Deficiencies or excesses can cause anemia, poor growth, strange appetite, fractures, convulsions, vomiting, weakness, heart problems, and many other disorders. Again, most commercial dog foods have minerals added in their ideal percentages. It is not a good idea to supplement your dog's diet with minerals, especially calcium.

Fiber: Fiber, such as beet pulp or rice bran, should make up a small part of the dog's diet. It's often used in weight-loss diets to give the dog a full feeling, although its effectiveness is controversial. Too much fiber causes large stool volume and can impair the digestion of other nutrients.

Water: This is essential for life. It dissolves and transports other nutrients, helps regulate body temperature, and helps lubricate joints. Dehydration can cause or complicate many health problems. Keep a bowl of clean, cool water available for your Min Pin at all times.

Special Diets

Several diseases can be helped by feeding specially formulated diets. Such diets can greatly add to a sick dog's quantity and quality of life, but often, dogs grow tired of them quickly. By understanding what ingredients must be avoided in a particular illness, you may be able to include some treats in the diet as well.

Food allergies: Min Pins that are allergic to food ingredients are typically allergic to particular proteins. Beef and corn are common culprits. By feeding a bland diet of proteins the dog has never eaten, such as venison, duck, or rabbit, the allergic symptoms (which range from diarrhea to itchiness) should subside. If they do, ingredients are added back one by one until an ingredient is found that triggers the response. You may have to keep your dog on a diet of novel proteins forever—at least until she develops an allergy to it and you must move to another novel protein. Some hypoallergenic diets consist not of novel proteins, but of protein molecules that are too small to cause allergic reactions.

"What's for supper?"
The most nutritious diet
won't do your dog any
good if she won't eat it.
Good taste counts.

Urinary stones: Dogs that tend to form urinary stones may be helped by diets high in certain minerals. Such diets are also usually high-fiber diets. Because there are several types of urinary stones, your veterinarian can suggest which diet is appropriate.

Diabetes mellitus: Diabetic dogs need diets high in complex carbohydrates, and they need to be fed on a strict schedule.

Liver disease: Dogs with liver disease must eat in order to get better, but they should avoid meat and instead get their protein from milk (unless it causes diarrhea) or soy products. They need small meals of complex carbohydrates frequently throughout the day. Vitamin A and copper levels must be kept low.

Pancreatitis: Pancreatitis is often precipitated by a high-fat meal, especially in older fatter dogs. They need to be fed a low-fat diet to lessen the likelihood of recurrence.

Congestive heart failure: Dogs with heart failure require a low-sodium diet (balanced with potassium) in order to lower their blood pressure. This will help reduce the accumulation of fluid in the lungs or abdomen.

Kidney disease: Diets for kidney disease should have moderate quantities of high-quality protein. Proteins produce toxic wastes that impaired kidneys cannot clear, causing the dog to feel ill. By feeding higher-quality protein, such as eggs (especially egg whites), beef, or chicken, the fewest toxic by-products are produced in comparison to protein used. Lower levels of high-quality protein will make the dog feel better in advanced kidney failure. Controlling phosphorus, common in meats and cheeses, is an essential part of diet management. Sodium must also be kept low. Feeding a high-fat diet will add essential calories.

Prescription diets are available through your veterinarian for all these conditions. In addition, your veterinarian can give you recipes for home-prepared diets that meet these requirements.

Just as with people, good grooming encompasses hair, nail, and dental upkeep. Keeping your Min Pin looking his best also helps keep him feeling his best.

Specific Care

Coat and Skin Care

Even with his close hair, your Min Pin will need a short grooming session once or twice a week in order to keep his coat gleaming and healthy. Use a natural bristle brush to distribute the oils, a rubber bristle brush to remove dead hair, and a flea comb to remove fleas or fine debris.

Bathing

Min Pins rarely need bathing (in fact, wiping them thoroughly with a damp sponge will work wonders), but when bathing is necessary, it is best accomplished in a sink with a spray attachment.

Making your Min Pin bloom means keeping the coat, eyes, ears, teeth, and nails in top condition.

✔ Use warm water that would be comfortable for you if it were your bath.
✔ Place cotton balls in the dog's ears, and wash his entire body before starting on his head.
✔ Rinse the head with a sponge, followed by the rest of the body with the spray.

Shampoo: You will get better results with a shampoo made for dogs. Dog skin has a pH of 7.5, whereas human skin has a pH of 5.5; bathing in a shampoo formulated for the pH of human skin can lead to scaling and irritation.

Most shampoos will kill fleas even if not especially formulated as a flea shampoo, but none has any residual killing action on fleas. In addition, there are a variety of therapeutic shampoos for use with skin problems. Treatment includes moisturizing shampoos for dry scaly skin, antiseborrheic shampoos for excessive scales and dandruff, antimicrobials for damaged skin, and oatmeal-based antipruritics for itchy skin.

If you start grooming your Min Pin as a puppy, it will be easier to groom him or her as an adult. Grooming also provides a special bonding time for you and your dog.

Finally, no one should be without one of the shampoos that requires no water or rinsing. These are wonderful for puppies, emergencies, and bathing when time is limited. When

A flea comb has teeth so finely spaced that any fleas are trapped between them.

finished, dry the dog thoroughly and do not allow him to become chilled.

Nail Care

When you can hear the pitter-patter of clicking nails, that means that with every step the nails are hitting the floor, and when this happens, the bones of the foot are spread, causing discomfort and eventually splayed feet and lameness.

If dewclaws are left untrimmed, they can get caught more easily or actually loop around and grow into the dog's leg. You must prevent this by trimming your dog's nails every week or two.

Begin by handling the feet and nails daily, and then "tipping" the ends of your puppy's nails every week, taking special care not to cut the "quick" (the central core of blood vessels and nerve endings).

Many people find a scissors-type clipper easier to use on a toy dog than a guillotine nail clipper, but either type is acceptable. You may find it easiest to cut the nails with your Min Pin lying on his back in your lap, or you may have a helper hold your dog.

If you look at the bottoms of the nails, you will see a solid core culminating in a hollowed nail. Cut the tip up to the core, but not beyond.

Styptic powder: On occasion, you will slip up and cause the nail to bleed. This is best stopped by styptic powder, but if this is not available, dip the nail in flour or hold it to a wet tea bag. Be ready for your Min Pin to demand an apology!

Like people, dogs can be allergic to many things in their environment, including pollen, dust mites, and even food.

The "quick" of the nail consists of blood vessels surrounded by nerves. The nail becomes progressively less brittle as it gets closer to the quick, providing another cue about its location when cutting.

Skin Problems

Healthy coats depend on healthy skin. If your Min Pin has coat problems, they could be from allergies, parasites, or a number of other problems that your veterinarian can diagnose.

Allergies

Signs of allergies are typically reddened itchy skin, particularly around the ears, eyes, feet, forelegs, armpits, and abdomen. The dog may scratch and lick, and rub her torso or rump on furniture or rugs. Dogs most often exhibit allergies through skin symptoms. They can be allergic to inhaled allergens, things they come in contact with, foods, or fleas. The most common inhaled allergens are dander, pollen, dust, and mold.

A healthy coat of any color will shine.

FAD: The most common allergy among all dogs is flea allergy dermatitis (FAD), which is an allergic reaction to the saliva that a flea injects under the skin whenever it feeds. Not only does it cause intense itching in that area, but all over the dog, especially around the rump, legs, and paws. Even a single flea bite can cause severe reactions in allergic dogs.

Allergens can be isolated with a skin test in which small amounts of allergen extracts are injected under the skin, which is then monitored for reactions. Besides avoiding allergens, treatment with antihistamines, glucocorticoids, or hyposensitization may be effective.

Fleas: Most over-the-counter products are permethrin-based, which isn't resistant to water and doesn't kill fleas for long. Flea populations can easily become resistant to it. In fact, fleas can become resistant to any treatment, so the best strategy is to change products frequently and to include the use of both a flea killer and a flea egg killer. Your veterinarian is the source of the most effective products for fighting fleas. Look for products containing one of the following ingredients:

• Imidacloprid: a self-distributing liquid that kills fleas within a day and continues for a month. It can withstand water, but not repeated bathing.

• Fipronil: a spray or self-distributing liquid that collects in the hair follicles and wicks out over time. It kills fleas for up to three months and ticks for a shorter time, and is resistant to bathing.

• Selamectin: a self-distributing liquid that kills fleas for one month. It also kills ear mites and several internal parasites, and acts as a heartworm preventive.

• Nytenpyram: an oral medication that starts killing fleas in 20 minutes; all fleas are killed in four hours. It has almost no residual activity, so it's mostly for a quick fix of heavily infested dogs.

• Lufenuron, methoprene, or fenoxycarb: chemicals that interfere with the hatching of flea eggs.

Ticks: Ticks are tough to kill. Fortunately, they are easy to spot on Min Pins. Fipronil flea products will kill ticks, but not immediately. Amitraz tick collars are also effective, but not perfect. To remove a tick, use a tissue or tweezers and grasp the tick as close to the skin as possible. Pull slowly, trying not to lose the head or squeeze the contents back into the dog. Even if you get the head with the tick, it will often leave a bump for several days.

Ticks can transmit several diseases. A vaccination is available for Lyme disease, but it's not advisable for dogs that don't live in Lyme endemic areas. Of greater concern is erhlichiosis, a potentially fatal disease that cripples the immune system and often has vague symptoms. Other tick-borne diseases include Rocky Mountain Spotted Fever and babesiosis. Your veterinarian can order blood tests if these conditions are suspected.

Mites: Mites can also cause problems. Sarcoptic mites cause sarcoptic mange, an intensely itchy disorder that you can catch. It's often characterized by small bumps and crusts on the ear tips, abdomen, elbows, and hocks. The condition can be treated with repeated shampoos or with an injection.

Demodex mites cause demodectic mange, a condition that is noncontagious but often difficult to treat. A couple of small patches in a puppy are commonplace and will usually go away on their own, but many such patches or a generalized condition must be treated with repeated dips or with drug therapy. Cases involving the feet can be especially difficult to cure.

Not everybody likes his or her ears cleaned!

Ear Care

You should examine both inside and outside your Min Pin's ears during your grooming session. Fly bites can sometimes irritate the outer edges, and can be treated with a soothing cream.

Dirt and wax: The ears may have an accumulation of dirt and wax. This can be removed by soaking a cotton ball with mineral oil and swabbing the ear. Do not reach farther than you can see. Do not use alcohol, which can dry and irritate the ear. Avoid also ear powders, which can cake in the ear. Ear cleaners, available from your veterinarian, are the best solution for maintaining ear health. If the ear continues to have an excessive discharge, it may be due to a fungal or bacterial problem, which must be treated by your veterinarian. It could also be due to ear mites.

Ear mites: Tiny but irritating, ear mites are highly contagious and often found in puppies. Affected dogs will shake their head, scratch their ears, and carry their head sideways. There is a dark waxy buildup in the ear canal, usually of both ears. If you place some of this wax on a piece of dark paper, and have very good eyes, you may be able to see tiny white moving specks. These are the culprits. Although there are over-the-counter ear mite preparations, they can cause worse irritation. Therefore, ear mites should be diagnosed and treated by your veterinarian.

Dental Care

At around five to six months of age, your Min Pin puppy will begin to shed its baby teeth and show off new permanent teeth. Often baby teeth, especially the canines ("fangs"), are not shed, so that the permanent tooth grows in beside the baby tooth. If this condition persists for over a week, consult your veterinarian. Retained baby teeth can cause misalignment of adult teeth.

Plaque: As your dog gets older, his teeth will tend to accumulate plaque. The plaque can be removed by brushing the dog's teeth once or twice weekly with a child's toothbrush and doggy toothpaste. You can also rub the teeth with hydrogen peroxide or a baking soda solution on a gauze pad to help remove tartar.

Hard dog foods and chew bones are helpful, but cannot do the job on their own. If not removed, plaque will attract bacteria and minerals, which will harden into tartar. If you cannot brush, your veterinarian can supply a cleansing solution that will help to kill plaque-forming bacteria, as well as bad breath! Neglected plaque and tartar can cause infections to form along the gum line. The infection can gradually work its way down the sides of the tooth until the entire root is undermined. The tissues and bone around the tooth erode, and the tooth finally falls out. Meanwhile, the bacteria may have been picked up by the bloodstream and carried throughout the body, causing infection in the kidneys and heart valves. Thicker tartar deposits will have to be removed with a dental

Check your Min Pin's teeth for correct scissors bite (as illustrated) and for tartar. Tooth problems can cause discomfort and serious health problems.

TIP

Correct Bite

Check the way your puppy's teeth meet up; in a correct bite, the bottom incisors should touch the back of the top incisors when the mouth is closed. Deviations from this can cause chewing problems and discomfort. Extreme deviations may need to be examined by a veterinarian.

scraper, possibly under anesthesia, which entails some risk in older Min Pins.

Note: Small dogs, including Min Pins, are especially prone to tooth loss and periodontal disease. There is no such thing as doggy dentures, so help your Min Pin keep his teeth into old age by keeping them sparkling throughout his life.

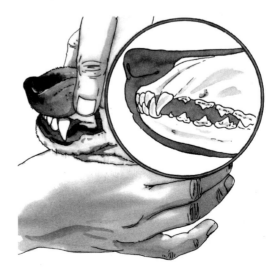

IN SICKNESS AND IN HEALTH

You are your Min Pin's first line of defense against illness. You're in charge of seeing that she receives the preventive medicine she deserves, for picking up signs of illness, for making the decisions in health care that are best for your dog, and for playing nurse when she needs home care.

Signs of Sickness

An abnormally quiet Min Pin may be a sick Min Pin. Possible causes include

✔ Infection (check for fever)

✔ Anemia (check gum color)

✔ Circulatory problem (check pulse and gum color)

✔ Pain (check limbs, neck, back, mouth, eyes, ears, and abdomen for signs)

✔ Nausea

✔ Poisoning (check gum color and pupil reaction; look for vomiting or abdominal pain)

✔ Sudden vision loss

✔ Cancer

✔ Metabolic diseases

Good health is the culmination of good genes, good care, and good luck. Good care is where you come in.

Sick dogs often lie quietly in a curled position. Dogs in pain may be irritable and restless, and may hide, pant, claw, and tremble. Dogs with abdominal pain often stretch and bow. A dog with breathing difficulties will often refuse to lie down or if she does, will keep her head raised. Confusion, head pressing, or seizures may indicate neurological problems.

Temperature, Pulse, and Hydration

Temperature: To take your dog's temperature, lubricate a rectal thermometer and insert it about 2 inches (5 cm) into the dog's anus, leaving it there for about a minute. Normal is from 101 to 102°F (38.3–38.9°C). If the temperature is

• 103°F (39.4°C) or above, call your veterinarian for advice. This is not usually an emergency.

• 105°F (40.5°C) or above, go to your veterinarian. This is probably an emergency;

Medications

Giving medications to your Min Pin should not be difficult. For pills, open your dog's mouth and place (don't throw) the pill well to the back and in the middle of the tongue. Close the mouth and gently stroke the throat until your dog swallows. Prewetting capsules or covering them with cream cheese or some other food helps prevent capsules from sticking to the tongue or the roof of the mouth.

For liquid medicine, tilt the head back and place the liquid in the pouch of the cheek. Then close your dog's mouth until she swallows. Always give the full course of medications prescribed by your veterinarian.

Sick dogs tend to sleep more. Of course, all dogs (even Min Pins) sleep. Get to know what's normal for your dog.

106° (41.1°C) or above is dangerous. Try to cool your dog.

• 98°F (36.6°C) or below, call your veterinarian for advice. Try to warm your dog.

• 96°F (35.5°C) or below, go to your veterinarian. Treat for hypothermia on the way by warming your dog.

Pulse: To check the pulse, cup your hand around the top of your dog's rear leg so your fingers are near the top, almost where the leg joins the body. Feel for the pulse in the femoral artery. Small dogs have faster pulses. Normal adult Min Pin pulse rate is 160 to 190 beats per minute; puppies are faster.

Hydration: Check hydration by touching the gums, which should be slick, not sticky, or by lifting the skin on the back and letting it go. It should snap back into place quickly, not remain tented. Sticky gums and tented skin indicate dehydration. If your dog has been vomiting or has diarrhea, she may instantly lose any water you give her, in which case your veterinarian may need to give your dog fluids under the skin, or better, in a vein.

Breed–Specific Health Problems

Every breed of dog comes from a closed gene pool based upon a limited number of foundation stock. Just as with people, every single dog carries on average five or so recessive genes for a deleterious health condition. When you close the breeding pool, you force descendants of these dogs to eventually interbreed with one another, which increases the chance that an offspring will end up inheriting the same recessive gene from both its sire and dam. When that happens, that offspring will exhibit that

The Five-Minute Checkup

Make several copies of this checklist and keep a record of your dog's home exams.

Date: _____

Weight: _____

Temperature: _____

Pulse: _____

Behavior

Is your dog
- ☐ Restless? ☐ Lethargic?
- ☐ Weak? ☐ Dizzy?
- ☐ Irritable? ☐ Confused?
- ☐ Bumping into things?
- ☐ Trembling? ☐ Pacing?
- ☐ Hiding?
- ☐ Eating more or less than usual?
- ☐ Drinking more than usual?
- ☐ Urinating more or less than usual, or with straining?
- ☐ Having diarrhea?
- ☐ Straining to defecate?
- ☐ Just standing with front feet on ground and rear in the air?
- ☐ Vomiting or trying to vomit?
- ☐ Regurgitating undigested food?
- ☐ Gagging? ☐ Coughing?
- ☐ Breathing rapidly at rest?
- ☐ Spitting up froth?
- ☐ Pawing at throat?
- ☐ Snorting?
- ☐ Limping?

Physical Exam

Hydration: ☐ Dry sticky gums?
  ☐ Skin that doesn't pop back when stretched?

Gum color: ☐ Pink (good) ☐ Bright red
  ☐ Bluish ☐ Whitish ☐ Red spots

Gums: ☐ Swellings? ☐ Bleeding?
  ☐ Sores? ☐ Growths?

Teeth: ☐ Loose? ☐ Painful? ☐ Dirty?
  ☐ Bad breath?

Nose: ☐ Thick or colored discharge?
  ☐ Cracking? ☐ Pinched? ☐ Sores?

Eyes: ☐ Tearing? ☐ Mucous discharge?
  ☐ Dull surface? ☐ Squinting?
  ☐ Swelling? ☐ Redness?
  ☐ Unequal pupils? ☐ Pawing at eyes?

Ears: ☐ Bad smell? ☐ Redness?
  ☐ Abundant debris? ☐ Scabby ear tips?
  ☐ Head shaking? ☐ Head tilt?
  ☐ Ear scratching? ☐ Painfulness?

Feet: ☐ Long or split nails? ☐ Cut pads?
  ☐ Swollen or misaligned toes?

Skin: ☐ Parasites? ☐ Black grains (flea dirt)?
  ☐ Hair loss? ☐ Scabs?
  ☐ Greasy patches? ☐ Bad odor?
  ☐ Lumps?

Anal and genital regions:
  ☐ Swelling? ☐ Discharge?
  ☐ Redness? ☐ Bloody urine?
  ☐ Bloody or blackened diarrhea?
  ☐ Worms in stool or around anus?
  ☐ Scooting rear?
  ☐ Licking rear?

Abdomen: ☐ Bloating?

Body: ☐ Asymmetrical bones or muscles?
  ☐ Lumps? ☐ Weight change?

The ability to enjoy life to its fullest depends to a large extent on having healthy joints.

health disorder. Because each breed starts with a different assortment of founders, each breed tends to be predisposed to a different set of health disorders.

Min Pins were lucky. As with all breeds, they do have some hereditary health problems. They have relatively few, however, and none that are extremely serious. Nonetheless, any Min Pin owner or breeder should be aware of Min Pin predispositions, especially Legg-Calve-Perthes disease, mucopolysaccharidosis, and patellar luxation.

LCPD

Legg-Calvé-Perthes disease (LCPD) is a disorder of one or both hip joints in which the blood supply to the femoral head is temporarily interrupted, usually some time between three and four months of age. The lack of blood causes the bone cells to die, which eventually causes the head of the femur to become disfigured or to collapse. When the disfigured femoral head no longer fits well into the hip socket, it causes varying degrees of lameness, stiffness, and pain. If it goes untreated, and the dog favors the leg enough, the muscle may atrophy.

Treatment: In mild cases, LCPD is treated by complete rest, preferably with the dog's affected leg (if only one) in a sling, for weeks or even months, to allow the damaged bone to reform. In more severe cases the disfigured femoral head must be surgically removed to relieve the pain. With time, muscle and other tissues tighten sufficiently around the hip socket to form a functional joint so that the dog doesn't even limp.

Diagnosis: Any case of rear leg lameness in a young Min Pin that lasts a week or more is suspect. Your veterinarian can diagnose LCPD with radiographs. Because LCPD is thought to have a genetic component, it's suggested that affected dogs not be bred. The Orthopedic Foundation for Animals (OFA) maintains an LCPD database.

MPS

Mucopolysaccharidosis (MPS) is a type of lysosomal storage disease, which means the body lacks a certain enzyme to break down certain large sugars, or polysaccharides. Different breeds have different forms of MPS; in Min Pins it is MPS VI, which means their deficient enzyme is one called arylsulfatase B, which is responsible for breaking down dermatin sulfate. This causes an accumulatioin of this substance in the cells, leading to skeletal deformities, especially of the hip joints, sternum, and vertebrae.

Symptoms: They may have stunted growth, clouded corneas, enlarged tongue, and possible heart problems from thickened heart valves. The corneal clouding may be evident as early as eight weeks of age, and most other signs by four months of age. The problems, especially the joint problems, become worse with age, and without treatment, most affected dogs die by three years of age.

Treatment: Treatment is possible, but it is expensive and experimental. It requires a bone marrow transplant from a clear dog, preferably a littermate, to provide white blood cells with the missing enzyme. If performed in a young puppy, the dog has a good possibility of leading a near normal life.

MPS VI is inherited as a simple recessive gene. A DNA test is available that can detect affected, carrier, and clear Min Pins (see *www.vet.upenn.edu/penngen* for testing details).

Patellar Luxation

Patellar luxation is a common problem of small dogs in which the patella, or kneecap, of

Min Pins are magnets for mischief. Put anything you don't want in your Min Pin's stomach out of reach!

Don't let your puppy up on things from which he could fall or jump.

one or both rear legs slips out of position. Normally, the patella slides up and down in a small groove (the trochlear groove) of the femur (thighbone) as the knee moves. It's secured in that groove not only by the deepness of the groove but by the tendon of the quadriceps muscle and by the joint capsule. In some dogs, the groove is too shallow or the muscle exerts too much rotational pull, allowing the patella to ride over the ridge of the groove. Once out of place (luxated), the muscle must relax before it can pop back into place. Relaxing the muscle means the leg must be straightened at the knee, so the dog will often hop for a few steps

with the leg held straight until the patella pops back into place. This hurts, so the dog may yelp. It also wears down the ridge, causing the condition to get gradually worse.

The condition may occur in one or both legs, and the patella may be displaced toward the outside of the leg or more commonly, the inside (which can give a bowlegged appearance). Signs are usually apparent by six months of age. Early diagnosis is helpful in slowing the progress, but treatment depends on what grade severity it is.

✔ Grade 1: The dog may occasionally skip, holding one hind leg forward for a step or two. The patella returns to its correct position easily.

✔ Grade 2: The dog often holds the affected leg up when moving, and the patella may not slide back into position by itself.

✔ Grade 3: The patella is usually out of position, slipping back out almost as soon as it is replaced. The dog only sometimes uses the affected leg.

✔ Grade 4: The patella is always out of position and cannot be replaced manually. The dog never puts weight on the leg.

Treatment: If your Min Pin has Grade 1 or 2 luxation, you may be able to slow the progress by keeping the dog's weight down, and keeping the muscle tone up with steady walking. Glucosamine supplements may help to build cartilage. Surgery to reconstruct the soft tissue surrounding the patella may prevent further progress if done early enough.

Grades 3 and 4 can be quite painful and cannot be treated conservatively. Surgery to tighten any stretched tissues and reconstruct the groove or realign the muscle will improve the condition, but may not return the leg to perfect. An orthopedic specialist has the best chance of success.

Common Problems

Min Pins also have the same signs of illness common to any dog, and chances are you'll eventually be confronted with some of them. Many of these are minor, but some can signal major problems as well.

Vomiting

Vomiting is a common occurrence that may or may not indicate a serious problem. You should consult your veterinarian immediately if your dog vomits a foul substance resembling fecal matter (indicating a blockage in the intestinal tract), blood (partially digested blood resembles coffee grounds), or if there is projectile vomiting, in which the stomach contents are forcibly ejected up to a distance of several feet. Sporadic vomiting with poor appetite and generally poor condition could indicate worms or a more serious internal disease that should also be checked by your veterinarian.

Causes: Overeating is a common cause of vomiting in puppies, especially if they follow eating with playing. Feed smaller meals more frequently if this becomes a problem.

Vomiting after eating grass is common and usually of no great concern.

Repeated vomiting could indicate that the dog has eaten spoiled food, undigestible objects, or may have stomach illness. Use the same home treatment as that outlined for diarrhea on the following page.

Diarrhea

Diarrhea can result from overexcitement or nervousness, a change in diet or water, sensitivity to certain foods, overeating, intestinal parasites, infectious diseases such as parvovirus or coronavirus, or ingestion of toxic substances.

Bloody diarrhea, diarrhea with vomiting, fever, or other signs of toxicity, or diarrhea that lasts for more than a day should not be allowed to continue without veterinary advice.

Treatment: Less severe diarrhea can be treated at home by withholding or severely restricting food and water. Ice cubes can be given to satisfy thirst. Administer a human antidiarrheal medicine in the same weight dosage as recommended for humans. A bland diet consisting of rice (flavored if need be with cooked, drained hamburger), cottage cheese, or cooked macaroni should be given for several days.

Intestinal Parasites

When you take the puppy to be vaccinated, bring along a stool specimen so that your veterinarian can also check for worms. Most puppies do have worms at some point, even

Heartworm larva are spread by mosquitoes from dog to dog. Untreated, they mature and reproduce in the infected dog's heart and can eventually cause death.

puppies from the most fastidious breeders. This is because some types of worms become encysted in the dam's body long before she ever becomes pregnant; perhaps when she herself is a puppy. Here they lie dormant and immune from worming, until hormonal changes due to her pregnancy cause them to be activated, and then they infect her babies.

You may be tempted to pick up some worm medication and worm your puppy yourself. Don't. Over-the-counter wormers are largely ineffective and often more dangerous than those available from your veterinarian. Left untreated, worms can cause vomiting, diarrhea, dull coat, listlessness, anemia, and death. Some heartworm preventives also prevent most types of intestinal worms, so that if you have a recurring problem in an older dog, they might help.

Tapeworms: Tapeworms tend to plague some dogs throughout their lives. There is no preventive, except to diligently rid your Min Pin of fleas, because fleas can transmit tapeworms to dogs. Tapeworms look like moving flat white worms on fresh stools, or may dry up and look like rice grains around the dog's anus.

Common misconceptions about worms exist. These include

✔ **Misconception:** A dog that is scooting her rear along the ground has worms. This is seldom the case; such a dog more likely has impacted anal sacs.

✔ **Misconception:** Feeding a dog sugar and sweets will give her worms. There are good reasons not to feed a dog sweets, but worms have nothing to do with them.

✔ **Misconception:** Dogs should be regularly wormed every month or so. Dogs should be wormed when, and only when, they have been diagnosed with worms. No worm medication is

completely without risk, and it is foolish to use it carelessly.

Impacted Anal Sacs

Dogs have two anal sacs that are normally emptied by rectal pressure during defecation. Their musky smelling contents may also be forcibly ejected when a dog is extremely frightened. Sometimes they fail to empty properly and become impacted or infected. This is more common in small dogs, obese dogs, dogs with seborrhea, and dogs that seldom have firm stools. Constant licking of the anus or scooting of the anus along the ground are characteristic signs of anal sac impaction. Not only is this an extremely uncomfortable condition for your dog, but left unattended, the impacted sacs can become infected. Your veterinarian can show you how to empty the anal sacs yourself. Some dogs may never need to have their anal sacs expressed, but others may need regular attention.

Urinary Tract Diseases

If your dog drinks and urinates more than usual, she may be suffering from a kidney problem. See your veterinarian for a proper diagnosis and treatment. Although the excessive urination may cause problems in keeping your house clean or your night's sleep intact, never try to restrict water from a dog with kidney disease. Untreated kidney disease can lead to death. Increased thirst and urination could also be a sign of diabetes.

Symptoms: If your dog has difficulty or pain in urination, urinates suddenly but in small amounts, or passes cloudy or bloody urine, she may be suffering from a problem of the bladder, urethra, or prostate.

Treatment: Your veterinarian will need to examine your Min Pin to determine the exact

Check the eyes daily. Eye problems
are not wait-and-see situations.

nature of the problem. Bladder infections must be treated promptly to avoid the infection reaching the kidneys. A common cause of urinary incontinence in older spayed females is lack of estrogen, which can be treated. Your veterinarian should check your older male's prostate to ensure that it is not overly enlarged, which can cause problems in both urination and defecation.

Coughing

Any persistent cough should be checked by your veterinarian. Coughing irritates the throat and can lead to secondary infections if allowed to continue unchecked. There are many reasons for coughing, including allergies, but two of the most common are kennel cough and heart disease.

Kennel cough: Kennel cough is a highly communicable airborne disease against which you can also request your dog be vaccinated. This is an especially good idea if you plan to have your dog around other dogs at training classes or while being boarded.

Heart disease can result in coughing following exercise or in the evening.

Treatment: Treatment with diuretics prescribed by your veterinarian can help alleviate the coughing for awhile, as can a special diet and other medications.

Eye Discharge

A watery discharge, accompanied by squinting or pawing, often indicates a foreign body in the eye. Examine under the lids and use a moist cotton swab to removed any debris. Flooding the eye with saline solution can also aid in

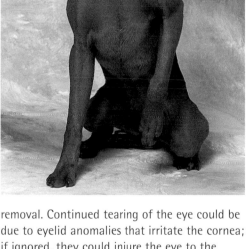

removal. Continued tearing of the eye could be due to eyelid anomalies that irritate the cornea; if ignored, they could injure the eye to the point of causing blindness.

Conjunctivitis: A thick or crusty discharge suggests conjunctivitis. Mild cases can be treated by over-the-counter preparations for humans, but if you don't see improvement within a day of treatment, your veterinarian should be consulted.

Note: Any time your dog's pupils do not react to light or when one eye reacts differently

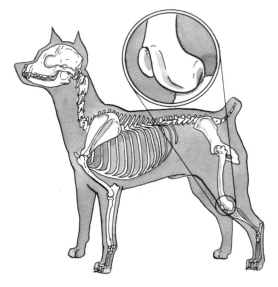

The Miniature Pinscher skeleton, with an enlarged view of the patella, the site of patellar luxation. Femoral head necrosis, another cause of lameness, occurs at the end of the thigh (femur) bone where it meets the pelvis.

from another, take your pet to the veterinarian immediately. It could indicate a serious ocular or neurological problem.

Limping

Puppies are especially susceptible to bone and joint injuries, and should not be encouraged to jump off of high places, walk on their hind legs, or run until exhausted. Persistent limping in puppies may result from one of several developmental bone problems, and should be checked.

Both puppies and adults should be kept off of slippery floors that could cause them to lose their footing. Limping may or may not indicate

a serious problem. When associated with extreme pain, fever, swelling, discoloration, deformity, or grinding or popping sounds, you should have your veterinarian examine your Min Pin at once.

• Ice packs may help minimize swelling if applied immediately after an injury.

• Fractures should be immobilized by splinting above and below the site of fracture (small rolled magazines work well on legs) before moving the dog.

• Mild lameness should be treated by complete rest; if it still persists after three days, your dog will need to be examined by its doctor.

• Knee injuries are common in dogs; most do not get well on their own.

• Avoid pain medications that might encourage the use of an injured limb.

Arthritis: In older dogs, or dogs with a previous injury, limping is often the result of arthritis. Arthritis can be treated with aspirin, but should be done so only under veterinary supervision. Do not use ibuprofen or naproxen. Any time a young or middle-aged dog shows signs of arthritis, especially in a joint that has not been previously injured, she should be examined by her veterinarian.

Breeding

One of the most unfortunate aspects of dog ownership is the compulsion so many people have to breed a litter. Rarely is this done with any foresight or responsibility, and the result, most often, is a grave disservice to themselves, their pets, the breed, and the resulting puppies.

Unless you have studied the breed, have proven your female to be a superior specimen in terms of conformation, health, and temperament, and plan to take responsibility for each and every puppy for the rest of her life, you have no business doing anything but having your dog neutered. Keep in mind:

✔ A litter is extremely expensive! Stud fee, prenatal care, whelping complications, cesarean sections, supplemental feeding, puppy food, vaccinations, advertising, and a staggering investment of time and energy are all involved.

✔ There is definite discomfort and a certain amount of danger to any dog, but especially a very small dog, when whelping a litter. Watching a litter be born is not a good way to teach the children the miracle of life; there are too many things that can go very wrong.

✔ A spayed female is far less likely to develop breast cancer and a number of other hormone-related diseases. She should be spayed before her first season in order to avoid these problems.

✔ Serious breeders have spent years researching genetics and the breed; they breed only the best specimens, and screen for hereditary defects in order to obtain superior puppies. Until you have done the same, you are undoing the hard work of those who have dedicated their lives to bettering the breed.

✔ Finding responsible buyers is very, very difficult, and you may find yourself at wit's end caring for a houseful of Min Pin juvenile delinquents. You may find homes, but will they really be good homes?

✔ There are many more purebred Miniature Pinschers in the world than there are good homes for them. The puppy you sell to a less-than-perfect buyer may end up neglected or discarded, or used to produce puppies to sell to even less desirable homes. Millions of purebreds are euthanized each year at pounds. Sometimes they are the lucky ones.

While breeding your dog is tempting, bear in mind that it's a lot of work and a huge responsibility.

✔ The fact that your Min Pin is purebred and registered does not mean it is breeding-quality, anymore than the fact that you have a driver's license qualifies you to build race cars. Everyone thinks his or her own dog is special, and she is. But that doesn't mean she should be bred.

✔ You will be unpleasantly surprised at the number of friends who just "had to have one of Greta's puppies" who will suddenly disappear from your life, develop allergies, or otherwise opt out of taking a puppy when the time comes.

The Very Mature Min Pin

With good care and good luck your Min Pin will mature and eventually, grow old—most Min Pins live to 12 to 14 years of age. Pat yourself on the back for a job well done, but be ready to

Older dogs like to take things at a slower pace—which still may not be all that slow.

Eyes and ears: Older dogs may seem to ignore their owners' commands, but this may be the result of hearing loss. The slight haziness that appears in the older dog's pupils is normal and has minimal effect upon vision, but some dogs, especially those with diabetes, may develop cataracts. These can be removed by a veterinary ophthalmologist if they are severe.

Activities and diet: Both physical activity and metabolic rates decrease in older animals, meaning that they require fewer calories to maintain the same weight. It is important to keep your older dog active. Older dogs that continue to be fed the same as when they were young risk becoming obese; such dogs have a greater risk of cardiovascular and joint problems.

Older dogs should be fed several small meals instead of one large meal, and should be fed on time. There are a variety of reduced calorie, low-protein senior diets on the market. But most older dogs do not require a special diet unless they have a particular medical need for it (such as obesity: low-calorie; kidney failure: low-protein; heart failure: low-sodium). Dogs with these problems may require special prescription dog foods, available from your veterinarian, that better address their needs.

Skin moisture: Like people, dogs lose skin moisture as they age, and though dogs don't wrinkle, their skin can become dry and itchy as a result. Regular brushing can stimulate oil production.

Odor: Older dogs tend to have a stronger body odor, but don't just ignore increased odors; they could indicate specific problems, such as periodontal disease, impacted anal sacs,

be twice as diligent in caring for your dog now. When does old age start? It varies between breeds and individuals, with the average Min Pin showing signs of aging at a much older age than most larger breeds do.

You may first notice that your dog sleeps longer and more soundly than she did as a youngster. Upon awakening, she is slower to get going and may be stiff at first. She may be less eager to play and more content to lie in the sun (in other words, she may begin to act like a normal dog!). Some dogs become cranky and less patient, especially when dealing with puppies or boisterous children.

seborrhea, ear infections, or even kidney disease. Any strong odor should be checked by your veterinarian.

Immune system: There is evidence that the immune system may be less effective in older dogs. This means that it is increasingly important to shield your dog from infectious disease, chilling, overheating, and any stressful conditions.

Anesthesia risk: Older dogs present a somewhat greater anesthesia risk. Most of this increased risk can be negated, however, by first screening dogs with a complete medical workup.

The older Min Pin especially needs a soft, warm bed.

Trips and Stress

Long trips may be grueling, and boarding in a kennel may be extremely upsetting. Introduction of a puppy or new pet may be welcomed and may encourage your older dog to play, but if your dog is not used to other dogs, the newcomer will more likely be resented and may be an additional source of stress.

Changes

The older dog should see her veterinarian at least biyearly, but the owner must take responsibility for observing any health changes. Some of the more common changes, along with some of the more common conditions they may indicate in older dogs are

✔ Limping: arthritis, patellar luxation.

✔ Nasal discharge: tumor, periodontal disease.

✔ Coughing: heart disease, tracheal collapse, lung cancer.

✔ Difficulty eating: periodontal disease, oral tumors.

✔ Decreased appetite: kidney, liver, or heart disease, pancreatitis, cancer.

✔ Increased appetite: diabetes, Cushing's syndrome.

✔ Weight loss: heart, liver, or kidney disease, diabetes, cancer.

✔ Abdominal distension: heart or kidney disease, Cushing's syndrome, tumor.

✔ Increased urination: diabetes, kidney or liver disease, cystitis, Cushing's syndrome.

✔ Diarrhea: kidney or liver disease, pancreatitis.

The above list is by no means inclusive of all symptoms or problems they may indicate. Vomiting and diarrhea can signal many different problems; keep in mind that a small older dog cannot tolerate the dehydration that results from continued vomiting or diarrhea and you should not let it continue unchecked.

In general, any ailment that an older dog has is magnified in severity compared to the same symptoms in a younger dog. The owner of any older dog must be even more careful and attentive as his or her dog ages. Don't be lulled into a false sense of security just because you own a Miniature Pinscher. A long life depends upon good genes, good care, and good luck.

The following situations are all *life-threatening emergencies*. For all cases, administer the first aid treatment outlined and seek the nearest veterinary help *immediately*. Call the clinic first so that they can prepare.

In general:

✔ Make sure breathing passages are open. Loosen collar and check mouth and throat.

✔ Be calm and reassuring. A calm dog is less likely to go into shock.

✔ Move the dog as little and as gently as possible.

✔ If the dog is in pain, she may bite. Apply a makeshift muzzle with a bandage or tape. Do not muzzle if breathing difficulties are present.

Shock

Signs: Very pale gums, weakness, unresponsiveness, faint pulse, shivering.

Treatment: Keep the dog warm and calm; control any bleeding; check breathing, pulse, and consciousness, and treat these problems if needed.

Heatstroke

Signs: Rapid, loud breathing; abundant thick saliva, bright red mucous membranes, high rectal temperature. Later signs: unsteadiness, diarrhea, coma.

Treatment: Immediately cover the dog with towels soaked in cold water. Place the dog in a cool room or in front of a fan. If this treatment is not possible, immerse the dog in water. You *must* lower your dog's body temperature quickly (but do not lower it below 100°F [37.8°C]).

Breathing Difficulties

Signs: Gasping for breath with head extended, anxiety, weakness; advances to loss of consciousness, bluish tongue (exception: carbon monoxide poisoning causes bright red tongue).

Treatment: If not breathing, give mouth-to-nose respiration:

1. Open the dog's mouth, clear passage of secretions and foreign bodies.

2. Pull the dog's tongue forward.

3. Seal your mouth over the dog's nose and mouth, blow gently into the dog's nose for three seconds, then release.

4. Continue until the dog breathes on her own.

If due to drowning, turn the dog upside down, holding her by the hind legs, so that water can run out of her mouth. Then administer mouth-to-nose respiration, with the dog's head positioned lower than her lungs.

An emergency muzzle can be fashioned by crossing a strip of cloth or your leash around the snout and tying it behind the ears.

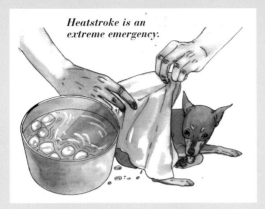

Heatstroke is an extreme emergency.

Apply pressure to wounds. Do not remove bandages even if they become saturated; instead, add new bandages on top of them.

Hypoglycemia (Low Blood Sugar)

Signs: Appears disoriented, weak, staggering. May appear blind, and muscles may twitch. Later stages lead to convulsions, coma, and death.

Treatment: Give food, or honey or syrup mixed with warm water.

Poisoning

Signs: Varies according to poison, but commonly include vomiting, convulsions, staggering, collapse.

Treatment: Call your veterinarian and give as much information as possible. Induce vomiting (except in the cases outlined below) by giving either hydrogen peroxide, salt water, or mustard and water. Treat for shock and get to the veterinarian at once. Be prepared for convulsions or respiratory distress.

Do *not* induce vomiting if the poison was an acid, alkali, petroleum product, solvent, cleaner, or tranquilizer, or if a sharp object was swallowed; also do *not* induce vomiting if the dog is severely depressed, convulsing, comatose, or if over two hours have passed since ingestion. If the dog is not convulsing or unconscious: dilute the poison by giving milk, vegetable oil, or egg whites.

Convulsions

Signs: Drooling, stiffness, muscle spasms.

Treatment: Prevent your dog from injuring herself on furniture or stairs. Remove other dogs from the area. Treat for shock.

Open Wounds

Signs: Consider wounds to be an emergency if there is profuse bleeding, if extremely deep, if open to chest cavity, abdominal cavity, or head.

Treatment: Control massive bleeding first. Cover the wound with a clean dressing and apply pressure; apply more dressings over the others until bleeding stops. Also, elevate the wound site, and apply a cold pack to the site. If an extremity, apply pressure to the closest pressure point as follows:

✔ For a front leg: inside of the front leg just above the elbow.

✔ For a rear leg: inside of the thigh where the femoral artery crosses the thighbone.

✔ For the tail: underside of the tail close to where it joins the body.

THE MIN PIN BLUEPRINT

What makes a champion? In the show ring, it is the adherence to a very exacting blueprint of the ideal Min Pin, known as the breed standard of perfection.

The Ideal Miniature Pinscher

No one dog ever fits the blueprint perfectly, but at the very least, a dog should fit it well enough so that she is easily recognized as a Miniature Pinscher. This possession of breed attributes is known as *type*, and is an important requirement of any purebred.

A dog should also be built in such a way that she can go about her daily life with minimal exertion and absence of lameness. This equally important attribute is known as *soundness*. Add to these the attributes of good health and temperament, and you have the four cornerstones of the ideal Miniature Pinscher.

"Characteristic traits are its hackneylike action, fearless animation, complete self-possession, and spirited presence." From the official Miniature Pinscher standard.

The AKC Miniature Pinscher Standard

General appearance: The Miniature Pinscher is structurally a well-balanced, sturdy, compact, short-coupled, smooth-coated dog. She naturally is well groomed, proud, vigorous, and alert. Characteristic traits are her hackney-like action, fearless animation, complete self-possession, and spirited presence.

Size, proportion, substance: Size: 10 to 12.5 inches (25.4–31.8 cm) in height allowed, with desired height 11 to 11.5 inches (27.9–29.2 cm) measured at the highest point of the shoulder blades. Disqualification: Under 10 inches (25.4 cm) or over 12.5 inches (31.8 cm) in height. Length of males equals height at the withers. Females may be slightly longer.

Gait: The forelegs and hind legs move parallel, with feet turning neither in nor out. The hackneylike action is a high-stepping, reaching, free and easy gait in which the front leg moves

The Min Pin is "structurally a well-balanced, sturdy, compact, short-coupled dog." From the official Miniature Pinscher standard.

straight forward and in front of the body and the foot bends at the wrist. The dog drives smoothly and strongly from the rear. The head and tail are carried high.

Coat: Smooth, hard, and short, closely adhering to the body.

Color:

• Solid clear red.

• Stag red (red with intermingling of black hairs).

• Black with sharply defined rust-red markings on cheeks, lips, lower jaw, throat, twin spots above eyes and chest, lower half of forelegs, inside of hind legs and vent region, lower portion of hocks and feet. Black pencil stripes on toes.

• Chocolate with rust-red markings the same as specified for blacks, except brown pencil stripes

"It naturally is well-groomed, proud, vigorous, and alert." From the official Miniature Pinscher standard.

The stylish high stepping hackney gait is an important and distinctive trait of the Miniature Pinscher.

Highlights of the Miniature Pinscher Standard

- **Head** tapering and narrow. Only a slight drop to the muzzle, which is parallel to the top of the skull.
- **Ears** erect and set high. May be cropped or uncropped.
- **Eyes** full, slightly oval, and dark (including eye rims).
- **Teeth** meet in scissors bite.
- **Neck** slightly arched, blending into shoulders, and muscular. No dewlap or throatiness.
- **Back** level or slightly sloping toward the rear, both when standing and gaiting.
- **Ribs** well sprung. Base of brisket level with point of elbow.
- **Belly** moderately tucked up.
- **Tail** set high, held erect, and docked.
- **Hocks** short.
- **Dewclaws** should be removed.
- **Feet** small and catlike; toes strong, well arched, and closely knit with deep pads and thick, blunt nails.

on toes. Chocolates have brown nose and lips, and lighter eyes.

Temperament: Fearless animation, complete self-possession, and spirited presence.

Disqualifications: Under 10 inches (25.4 cm) or over 12.5 inches (31.8 cm) in height. Any color other than listed. Thumb mark (patch of black hair surrounded by rust on the front of the foreleg between the foot and the wrist; on chocolates, the patch is chocolate hair). White on any part of the dog that exceeds 0.5 inch (1.3 cm) in its longest dimension.

INFORMATION

Organizations

American Kennel Club
260 Madison Avenue
New York, NY 10016
(212) 696-8200
www.akc.org

AKC Registration
5580 Centerview Drive
Raleigh, NC 27606
(919) 233-9767

Home Again Microchip System
1-800-LONELY ONE

Miniature Pinscher Club of America
Christine Filler, Secretary
35038 N. 10th Street
Desert Hills, AZ 85086
www.minpin.org
E-mail: MPCAsecretary@minpin.org

Rescue

Internet Miniature Pinscher Service—IMPS
(877) MIN-PIN1
www.minpinrescue.org

Miniature Pinscher Club of America
www.minpin.org/rescue.htm
E-mail: MPCARescue@minpin.org

Southern Star MinPin Rescue, Inc.
(866) 331-PINS
www.miniaturepinscherrescue.org

Books

Boshell, Buris R. *Your Miniature Pinscher.*
Fairfax, Virginia: Denlingers, 1969.
Coile, Caroline. *Congratulations! It's a Dog.*
Hauppauge, NY: Barron's Educational Series,
Inc., 2005.
_____. *Encyclopedia of Dog Breeds.* Hauppauge,
NY: Barron's Educational Series, Inc., 2005.
_____. *Show Me! A Dog-Showing Primer.*
Hauppauge, NY: Barron's Educational Series,
Inc., 1997.
Hungerland, Jaqueline. *The Miniature Pinscher:
Reigning King of Toys.* New York: Howell
Book House, 2000.
Krogh, David. *The King of Toys Champion Book.*
Gresham, Oregon: Garvin Lazertype.
Tietjen, Sari Brewster. *The New Miniature
Pinscher.* New York: Howell Book House,
MacMillan Publishing, 1988.
Wood, Deborah. *Little Dogs: Training Your
Pint-Sized Companion.* Neptune City, NJ: TFH.
2004.

*Min Pins are always up for an adventure—
sometimes, more of one than you had
in mind!*

Magazines

Pinscher Patter (available only to members of Miniature Pinscher Club of America).

Top Notch Toys
8848 Beverly Hills
Lakeland, FL 33809-1604
www.dmcg.com

Several all-breed magazines are listed at *www.dogchannel.com*

Video

Miniature Pinscher #VVT508
The American Kennel Club
Attn: Video Fulfillment
5580 Centerview Drive
Suite 200
Raleigh, NC 27606
(919) 233-9780
www.akc.org

A buckle collar is fine for training, and certainly better than a slip collar for everyday wear. Plus they can be fancy!

Web Sites

Canine Health Foundation
www.akcchf.org

Kennel Clubs Worldwide
http://henceforths.com/kennel_clubs.html

Orthopedic Foundation for Animals
www.offa.org

Therapy Dogs International
www.tdi-dog.org

Westminster Kennel Club
www.westminsterkennelclub.org

INDEX

About the Author

Caroline Coile is an award-winning author who has written articles about dogs for both scientific and lay publications. She holds a Ph.D. in the field of neuroscience and behavior, with special interests in canine sensory systems, genetics, and behavior. Her own dogs have been nationally ranked in conformation, obedience, agility, and field-trial competition.

Acknowledgments

Special thanks are due the many Miniature Pinscher owners and breeders who lent their expertise to this book, and to editors Seymour Weiss and Annemarie McNamara, as well as the rest of the staff at Barron's.

Cover Photos

Isabelle Francais: front cover and back cover; Isabelle Francais: Inside front cover and inside back cover.

Important Note

This pet owner's manual tells the reader how to buy or adopt, and care for, a Miniature Pinscher. The author and publisher consider it important to point out that the advice given in the book is meant primarily for normally developed dogs of excellent physical health and sound temperament.

Anyone who acquires a fully-grown dog should be aware that the animal has already formed its basic impressions of human beings. The new owner should observe the animal carefully, including its behavior toward humans, and, whenever possible, should meet the previous owner.

Caution is further advised in the association of children with dogs, in meeting with other dogs, and in exercising the dog without a leash.

These matters assume even greater importance when the dog is of a Toy breed.

Even well-behaved and carefully supervised dogs can sometimes damage property or cause accidents. It is therefore in the owner's interest to be adequately insured against such eventualities, and we strongly urge all dog owners to purchase a liability policy that also covers their dog.

Photo Credits

Norvia Behling: 23, 25, 29, 30, 31, 34, 36, 47, 58, 62, 70, 74, 77, 78, and 93; Kent Dannen: 4, 5, 13, 57, 60, 67, 76, 84, 90 (top), and 92; Tara Darling: 7, 8, and 63; Isabelle Francais: 2, 3, 9, 10, 11, 16, 17, 18, 19, 21, 22, 24, 28, 32, 33, 38, 42, 43, 44, 46, 48, 52, 56, 61, 64, 65, 66, 68, 72, 81, 83, 88, 89, and 90 (bottom); Pets by Paulette: 35, and 73.

© Copyright 2006, 1996 by Barron's Educational Series, Inc.

All inquiries should be addressed to:
Barron's Educational Series, Inc.
250 Wireless Boulevard
Hauppauge, NY 11788
www.barronseduc.com

ISBN-13: 978-0-7641-3397-8
ISBN-10: 0-7641-3397-7

Library of Congress Catalog Card No. 2006042845

Library of Congress Cataloging-in-Publication Data
Coile, D. Caroline.
  Miniature pinschers : everything about purchase, care, nutrition, behavior and training / D. Caroline Coile; illustrations by Michele Earle-Bridges.
     p. cm.
  Includes bibliographical references (p. 92) and index.
   ISBN-13: 978-0-7641-3397-8
   ISBN-10: 0-7641-3397-7
   1. Miniature pinscher. I. Title.

SF429.M56C65 2006
636.76—dc22   2006042845

Printed in China
9 8 7 6 5 4 3 2 1